The Political Thought of Jacques R

THE UNIVERSITY OF
WINCHESTER

Martial Rose Library
Tel: 01962 827306

2 6 NOV 2008

To be returned on or before the day marked above, subject to recall.

The Political Thought of Jacques Rancière

Creating Equality

Todd May

EDINBURGH UNIVERSITY PRESS

© Todd May, 2008

Edinburgh University Press Ltd
22 George Square, Edinburgh

Typeset in 11/13pt Adobe Sabon
by Servis Filmsetting Ltd, Manchester, and
printed and bound in Great Britain by
CPI Antony Rowe, Chippenham, Wilts

A CIP record for this book is available from the British Library

ISBN 978 0 7486 3532 0 (hardback)
ISBN 978 0 7486 3586 3 (paperback)

The right of Todd May
to be identified as author of this work
has been asserted in accordance with
the Copyright, Designs and Patents Act 1988.

Contents

Contents

Acknowledgements

Over the course of the conception and writing of this book I have accumulated several important debts. Peter Hallward introduced me to the thought of Jacques Rancière. Soon after, Phil Watts offered me the opportunity to present a paper at a conference that Rancière attended in Pittsburgh. Ian Buchanan promoted the project with Edinburgh University Press, and Carol MacDonald enthusiastically shepherded it through review and acceptance. Three anonymous readers for Edinburgh University Press offered timely and helpful comments. Jacques Rancière encouraged me throughout the book's writing. Parts of Chapter 4 have previously appeared as "Jacques Rancière and the Ethics of Equality" in *SubStance* and "Equality as a Foucaultian Value: The Relevance of Rancière" in *Philosophy Today*. I am grateful to The University of Wisconsin Press and to DePaul University respectively for permission to reprint these pieces here. Aside from this, one must acknowledge the courage of those who resist, in Palestine, in Chiapas, in Burma, in the U.S., and everywhere there is domination, which is to say, everywhere. They deserve more gratitude than I can give them, and more from the world than they are likely ever to receive.

This book is dedicated to Kathleen, David, Rachel, and Joel.

CHAPTER 1

Passive Equality

Ours is an age of political passivity. Not everywhere, nor among everyone. But in the United States, and among most of us. We are not utterly passive. After all, many (although not most) of us vote. We hold political opinions. We have expectations of our government. But we do not engage in political *action*. We do not organize; we neither create nor engage in political collectivities. We partake in politics as we do in sports, as fans rather than participants, and at times with rather less enthusiasm.

Why is this?

There are many reasons. The United States in particular is a large country. It is easy to feel as though one cannot make a difference politically. And layered upon this, there is the corruption of so much of mainstream politics. Who will listen to reason or values when the appeal of money seems so much to outweigh them? In a political system where leaders move seamlessly between legislating and lobbying, it is difficult to take seriously the power of what might quaintly be called the voice of the people.

And there is more. There is the individualism that is so much a part of U.S. ideology and that it is being exported with globalization: the view that success is to be had by dint of one's own efforts. To rely on others is a testimony to the failure of one's capacity to shape a personal future, to create oneself. To join with others in political action is not so much to enact a vision of collective life as it is to communalize one's personal complaints against the world. Political organizing is an exercise in weakness. All politics is, in the end, special interest politics. What I cannot do for myself I ask the government to do for me. The refusal of politics, then, is a sign of self-reliance.

I am concerned here with yet another reason for the failure of political action. It is related to individualism, and may, at least indirectly, give rise to a sense of impotence and even to corruption. But it is directly none of these. This reason is theoretical. It resides in how our political theories, our political philosophies, converge with these other reasons, and perhaps others still, to produce political passivity. I do not want to claim that theoretical deficiency underlies or overrides other contributions to this passivity. It is not that the fault lies in our theories rather than in ourselves. Rather, I want to focus on a single aspect of our political experience, the theoretical aspect, to see how it has gone wrong and how it might be corrected.

Many thinkers (Michel Foucault comes to mind as a recent example) have pointed to the complex interactions between how we think about ourselves and how we act. It is naïve, in the way that academics can be naïve, to hold that who we are is a product of our theories, that societies and cultures are determined by what intellectuals are thinking, or by what is taught in collegiate liberal arts and social science courses. But it is also naïve, in the way that those who are not engaged in intellectual pursuits can be naïve, to believe that societies and cultures are immune from those ideas, that they have no bearing upon the course of our individual and collective lives. If I choose to focus here on the theoretical contribution to our political passivity, it is because I believe that that contribution is neither singly determinative nor utterly marginal. It is one of many elements that must be reckoned with if we are to recover the project of political action. We must learn to act politically and to think in terms of political action. And to do this, it will help to have a political theory or a political philosophy that frames our political lives in terms of action rather than passivity.

I want to show, then, that mainstream political philosophy is a philosophy of political passivity. More specifically, I want to argue that it is a philosophy of passive equality. That is the first task, and it will take up this first chapter. But the most urgent task is not that of critique. To recognize the passivity of our theories is a ground-clearing operation. The real work is to build anew. The next four chapters are dedicated to that task. Chapter 2 appeals to the work of the French historian and thinker Jacques Rancière in order to build a framework for political thought that relies on active rather than passive equality. Chapter 3 relates that thought to its closest cousin, anarchism, showing not only how anarchism anticipates the thought of active equality, but also how the concept of equality as it is elaborated clarifies difficulties in anarchist thought. Chapter 4 seeks to construct a normative framework for that political thought. The final chapter turns toward our political situation, asking what contribution this new idea of political equality can make in thinking about and acting in the state of our current world.

From this quick sketch, you will undoubtedly recognize that the orientation of this political framework emerges from what is often called the "left." Indeed it does. In this day and in the U.S., the right does not have need of political action and still less of political action concerned with equality. We live in a society that is at once conservative and hierarchical. The left, by contrast, in much of the West, is in disarray. To act out of the presupposition of equality is to challenge our institutions and our political traditions in the name of those who are not its beneficiaries, of those who, in many ways and across many registers, remain outside or beneath the benefits that passive equality distributes. This book has little to offer those who believe themselves entitled to the resources or labor of others, nor to those who think that imposing one's military will upon others amounts to a justification of one's political convictions. It is, indeed, a critique of and an alternative to theories whose consequences have (often unintentionally) contributed to leading us to a situation where such entitlements can seem tolerable. It does so, I hope, as rigorously as it does unapologetically.

As a first task we need to come to an understanding of what *passive equality* means. Its nuances will be described over the course of this chapter. We might offer a preliminary definition of passive equality as the creation, preservation, or protection of equality by governmental institutions. The animating idea behind passive equality is that some form of equality is to be ensured by an institution for the sake of those whose equality is at stake. It is to be given, or at least protected, rather than taken or enacted by the subjects of equality.

This does not mean that the governing institution must give the actual equality itself. There are at least two other possibilities. First, there can already be some form of equality that people possess, or would naturally possess were they are not interfered with, and the institution's role is simply to preserve or protect that equality. This is the case where the equality at stake is that of liberty, as we shall see when we discuss Robert Nozick's libertarianism. Liberty is something that people are already capable of exercising; it does not need to be granted by the state. The role of the state is to ensure that it remains intact. Another possibility is that in order to ensure some form of equality, people have to be given *something else*, something other than equality. One might read aspects of the thought of John Rawls, also discussed later, as promoting things that ensure equality rather than giving equality directly. However, because these different ways of approaching equality share the characteristic that they place the subject of equality in the position of recipient rather than actor, they are both forms of passive equality.

The economist and Nobel Laureate Amartya Sen believes – correctly in my view – that some form of equality lies at the core of contemporary political philosophies. He writes, "a common characteristic of virtually all the approaches to the ethics of social arrangements that have stood the test of time is to want equality of *something* – something that has an important place in the particular theory."[1] For Sen, the issue that divides various philosophies of politics is the question of what it is that there should be equality of. Should there be equality of outcome, or resources, of liberty, of income, of opportunity, of happiness, some combination of these, or something else altogether? This is what political philosophers are really arguing about even when they cast their debates in other terms.

One of the virtues of this way of approaching political philosophy is that it reframes in a helpful way the stale debate between equality and liberty. Should there be liberty for people to do what they like, which will promote inequality among a society's members; or should there be equality, which would have to come at the expense of liberty? In Sen's hands, this question takes on a new guise. If we are to take people as equal and recognize the governing institutions as obliged to protect that equality, what role does equal liberty play in this, as opposed to other types of equality that might be considered important to the unfolding of human lives? Putting the question this way does not solve it, but it does allow us to approach it in a fresh way, one that perhaps opens up new avenues of thought.

We will not pursue those avenues here. All of them lie on the map of passive equality. For Sen, as for Nozick and Rawls, equality concerns what institutions are obliged to give people, rather than what those people themselves do politically. These three thinkers are oriented toward what people get as opposed to how they might act. This is at the heart of contemporary theories of justice and is indicated by the term used to describe them: distributive theories of justice.

Distributive theories of justice focus on the question of how the benefits and burdens of a society ought to be distributed. How should the goods a society possesses – its wealth, its health care, its jobs, its education, its resources, its rights – be distributed? And how should the burdens required by a society – its protection, the funding of its various goods, its burdensome jobs – be distributed? By asking these questions, one can immediately grasp that distributive theories of justice are concerned with passive equality. To put the point baldly for the moment, distributive theories of justice seek some form of equality that is to be recognized, and on the basis of this argue for a distribution of goods that will create, preserve, or protect that equality.

Theories of distributive justice have come in for much criticism, particularly from the left. Iris Marion Young, in her book *Justice and the Politics of Difference*, argues trenchantly that distributive theories of justice give an inordinate focus to material goods and see those goods as static and unchanging. By focusing on the allocation of material goods, theories of distributive justice "ignore the social structure and institutional context that often help determine distributive patterns."[2] In distributive theories of justice, the central issue becomes who has what rather than how people participate in the creation of their common lives. This neglects people's capacity for collective and autonomous action, and blunts the democratic character of political involvement.

Young notes that not all allocations have to be material. There can be allocations of rights or opportunities. "But," she notes, "this widening of the concept of distribution exhibits the second problem with the distributive paradigm. When metaphorically extended to nonmaterial social goods, the concept of distribution represents them as though they were static things, instead of a function of social relations and processes."[3] When one is concerned above all with distributions, one becomes blind to the political realm of power and its effects on people. In particular, theories of distributive justice neglect the twin problems of oppression and domination. Oppression, in young's view, "consists in systematic institutional processes which prevent some people from learning and using satisfying and expansive skills in socially recognized settings, or institutionalized social processes which inhibit people's ability to play and communicate with others or to express their feelings and perspective on social life." Whereas domination "consists in institutional conditions which inhibit or prevent people from participating in determining their actions or the conditions of their actions."[4] Oppression prevents people from displaying their capacities and domination prevents them from adequate participation in public life.

It might be thought that Young's criticisms of theories of distributive justice, particularly her criticism of its neglect of domination, are essentially a critique of theories of distributive justice as offering only passive equality. The view I want to present here, however, lies further along the road that Young's position begins to take. For Young, political action that resists domination requires participation in the creation of the institutional context in which one lives. For the perspective developed here, it lies in collective action itself. The institutional context is not the concern of what will be called here *democratic* action. This difference becomes evident when, later in this chapter, we discuss Young's own view and her positive proposals. It is possible to be against the distributive paradigm that Young criticizes and yet to remain bound to forms, albeit less egregious ones, of passive equality. Young's view may be seen as an instance, indeed a powerful one, of democratic socialism. The view defended here has deeper affinities with anarchism.

In approaching the critical task that constitutes the remainder of this chapter, I turn first to the liberalism of John Rawls and then to the libertarianism of Robert Nozick. Over thirty years after the appearance of the central texts of these thinkers, their debate remains central to the intellectual structure of mainstream political philosophy. Amartya Sen's revision of Rawls' theory will be the next concern. Sen offers a conception of political philosophy that sees people as more active in the construction of their lives than does Rawls. Finally, we turn to Iris Marion Young's view, one that stands at the threshold of Jacques Rancière's view offered in Chapter 2.

The task in all these cases is not one of offering exhaustive criticism of their views, nor is it to say that they have no bearing on the current political scene. Indeed, although something like Nozick's view is currently in the ascendant, the substitution of the views of Rawls, Sen, or Young would considerably improve our political situation. Moreover, the view defended here does not eliminate thinking in terms of distribution or participation in public life. It seeks to *move* those goals from the center to the margins of political thought rather than to *remove* them. My goal in this chapter is twofold. First, I would like to show how each of these theories endorses some form of passive equality. Second, I would like to suggest that thinking in terms of passive equality contributes to the passivity that pervades our political lives.

In his masterwork *A Theory of Justice*, Rawls does not shy away from placing his view squarely within the distributive paradigm. He tells us at the outset that, "For us the primary subject of justice is the basic structure of society, or more exactly, the way in which the major social institutions distribute fundamental rights and duties and determine the division of advantages from social cooperation."[5] A just social arrangement is one that determines the distribution in the appropriate way. The question for Rawls, as for every thinker of distributive justice, is, what is the proper distribution?

Rawls is aware of the dangers of a direct approach to that question. A direct approach would consist in offering a principle, or a set of principles, for determining how the distribution should be undertaken, and then proceeding to defend it. However, political and ethical intuitions do not form a tightly knit whole. Normative principles of justice and morality do not hang together in the same systematic way that scientific claims are supposed to. They are more diffuse, less engaged in the sense that the gears of a machine engage one another. As a result, one cannot start with a principle, defend it by means of other principles, facts, and moral intuitions, and then conclude with any confidence that one has arrived at a just distribution. Someone else could do much the same thing with a different, or perhaps even contradictory, set of principles and intuitions and arrive at a very different conclusion about the character of a just distribution.

If one is to recognize principles for a just distribution, then one cannot start with the principles themselves. Instead, the project must become one of starting with a *method* for generating a just set of principles. Then, if the method is adequate, the principles deriving from it will also be adequate. This way of approaching the normative arena of justice is like science in one particular respect. In science, if one agrees to the scientific method, one is thereby committed to the results of that method. With science, of course, that commitment is always defeasible should a different application of the method yield different results. But what one cannot do is to be committed to the adequacy of the scientific method and then reject what results from an application of the method. This is part (but only part) of the systematic character of science.[6]

The method Rawls employs is the famous veil of ignorance. One chooses whatever principles of distribution one likes for the society one is to live in, but has no knowledge of one's place or characteristics in that society. Race, religious belief (if any), physical advantages or handicaps, material status, personality characteristics, gender: these are all unknown to the person in the position (the *original* position, in Rawls' terminology) of choosing the principles of distribution for the society one is to occupy. The veil of ignorance forces an impartiality upon those who do the choosing, since it forces the chooser to take account of all the possible positions he or she could be assigned. It is impossible to privilege one's own interests in choosing distributive principles if one does not know what those interests are going to be.

Related to this, and more important for our purposes, is that the veil of ignorance, by imposing impartiality, also imposes a certain equality. Impartiality in the context of choosing distributive principles means precisely that the chooser must take all possible positions that can be occupied into equal account. This does not require that each possible position receives an equal amount or an equal benefit from the distribution. It might – and for Rawls *will* – turn out that it makes more sense to choose principles that favor people in certain positions rather than others. It might be better – that is, it might make more sense from the perspective from behind the veil of ignorance – to have principles that, under certain conditions, favor the poor over the rich, or the physically handicapped over the athletically gifted.

If so, this is not the result of *methodological* inequality. The method of the veil of ignorance requires all positions to be taken into account. Each possible position in the social order must receive equal consideration since one might occupy any of those positions. Rather, an inequality will be a result of recognizing that methodological equality may yield a certain inequality of distribution. Giving equal consideration or respect to every position one might occupy can result in an unequal distribution of the social goods. However, there are limits to inequalities of this kind. Those limits are circumscribed by the fact that, for instance, it is possible to be rich as well as poor. Therefore, any inequality favoring the poor cannot be given without undue consideration of its effects on the rich. In that sense, the methodological equality of the veil of ignorance is carried into the principles of distribution to be chosen.

The idea of methodological equality is founded in Rawls' conception of his version of justice as a Kantian one.

> Kant held, I believe, that a person is acting autonomously when the principles of his action are chosen by him as the most adequate possible expression of his nature as a free and equal rational being. The principles he acts upon are not adopted because of his social position or natural endowments, or in view of the particular kind of society in which he lives or the specific things he happens to want.[7]

The veil of ignorance in this sense corresponds to Kant's idea of purely rational beings. A purely rational being makes choices, not on the basis of particular interests or inclinations, but on the basis of the dictates of rationality alone.

Kantian ethics carves a sharp distinction between inclination, on the one hand, and duty or obligation, on the other. As Kant writes in the *Groundwork of the Metaphysic of Morals*, "[T]o preserve one's life is a duty, and besides this every one has also an immediate inclination to

To be sure, there will be people participating in this sequence. People will attend the constitutional convention, elect legislators, become administrators and judges. However, this is a far cry from the equal participation characteristic of equal rationality. In the original position, *anyone* is the subject of reflection. The power of the original position lies precisely in its invitation to anyone who is interested in reflecting on justice to participate in the formation of just principles. By contrast, in the sequence by which the principles are enacted in a particular society, only *some* people participate in the process. Their role is to represent, on the one hand, the principles of distributive justice, and on the other, all those people who will not be participating in the process.

Furthermore, even the participation of these few is not *in itself* a political good. The value of their participation does not lie in the fact that they are participating. To anticipate a formulation that will arise in Chapter 2, their participation is not an expression of their own equality. Rather, participation in the sequence Rawls describes is for the purpose of instantiating principles whose goal is the equal consideration of all citizens, that is, the meeting of legitimate expectations.

It might be pointed out here that, given the principles, the sequence Rawls describes is an appropriate one. If the goal is to meet the legitimate expectations of a populace, then the means toward that goal should be to create institutions that reflect those expectations. True, Rawls' view of the sequence of instantiating the principles is of a piece with the character of the principles themselves. From the perspective of active participation in politics, that is precisely the problem. From the moment the principles are formed, up to their instantiation in particular institutions, everything happens in accordance with equal consideration, with a passive equality to which people are entitled rather than an active equality in which they participate. There remains no trace, at the level of principles or of institutions, of the act of choosing which happens behind the veil of ignorance. As Rawls tells us, after choosing the principles, the choosers "return to their place in society." Participation in politics on the basis of equality ends with the decision about which principles are best suited to offer equal consideration to all members of one's society.

In recent mainstream contemporary philosophy, perhaps the greatest competitor to Rawls' view of justice is Robert Nozick's, and especially his *Anarchy, State, and Utopia*. Among the ruling classes in the Western world, Nozick's view has a certain appeal. Particularly with the advent (or at least the acceleration) of globalization, political views that criticize the interventions of governments in favor of the working of markets are in the ascendant. Governments are, as Ronald Reagan used to say, the problem rather than the solution. This view of the priority of markets over governments can be defended in at least two ways. The first, more common in contemporary thought, is that allowing capitalist markets to operate in an unfettered fashion will bring the greatest good to the greatest number of people. Encouraging individual initiative frees the creative resources of each member of a population, allows the efficient operation of supply and demand, and promotes peace through economic interaction such as trade. This view, while continuing to fare well as official ideology – it remains a central tenet of the Washington Consensus – has not fared quite as well empirically. It turns out that unfettered capitalist markets may be good for capitalists. It is less clear that they are good for anyone else.[14]

The second approach to defending capitalist markets against government intervention relies not on the general utility of these markets but on the rights of the participants in the markets. This approach is broadly Kantian rather than utilitarian. It is the approach Nozick takes. "In contrast to incorporating rights into the end state to be achieved, one might place them as side constraints upon the actions to be done: don't violate constraints C."[15] This view is distinct from Rawls', and as a consequence involves a different interpretation of Kantian requirements. Its difference from Rawls lies in its concern not for the results of a particular distribution, but for the process by which that distribution comes about. For Nozick, the core of justice is not an issue of who has what, but rather of how people go about interacting in a society. Because of this, Nozick's approach may at first glance seem like a more active approach to justice and ultimately to equality. It will turn out not to be.

Nozick, like Rawls, sees his approach to justice as Kantian. In doing so, he places the accent on a different point of Kant's thought from Rawls. For Rawls, it is equal consideration that forms the core of the Kantian approach to justice. If one is to decide justly for a society, she must remove herself from her particular interests and inclinations and decide on the basis of all interests and inclinations. This reflects the Kantian ideal of a purely rational being. Nozick's Kant is less interested in pure rationality than in treating people as ends rather than as means. "Side constraints upon action reflect the underlying Kantian principle that people are ends and not merely means; they may not be sacrificed or used for the achieving of other ends without their consent. Individuals are inviolable."[16] This, of course, is in keeping with the second formulation of Kant's categorical imperative: "*Act in such a way that you always treat humanity, whether in your own person or in the person of any other, never simply as a means, but always at the same time as an end.*"[17] Of course, like Rawls, Nozick is not simply interpreting Kant but enlisting him for a philosophical project that is different in orientation from Kant's. But his view of Kant as a proponent of side-constraints is a very different take on Kant's concept of autonomy from Rawls'.

It is not surprising, then, that Nozick challenges Rawls' formulation of the veil of ignorance, which is the centerpiece of Rawls' appropriation of Kant as a proponent of equal rationality.

> A procedure that founds principles of distributive justice on what rational persons who know nothing about themselves or their histories would agree to *guarantees that end-state principles of justice will be taken as fundamental* . . . no historical principle, it seems, could be agreed to in the first instance by the participants in Rawls' original position. For people meeting together behind a veil of ignorance to decide who gets what, knowing nothing about any special entitlements people may have, will treat anything to be distributed as manna from heaven.[18]

From behind the veil of ignorance, the goods to be distributed – particularly in the way of material resources and opportunities – appears to belong to nobody, to have no history. One is then free to offer any particular principles for arranging the distribution of those goods.

But goods have a history. People own them, they trade them or sell them or give them to others. The veil of ignorance is a methodological denial of this fact. It is a poor methodology, and so we must abandon it. How, then, are we to think of distributive justice if not through the methodological approach that Rawls has offered? Nozick suggests that we return to the Kantian core of treating people as ends rather than as means, and proposes that this return is tantamount to placing side-constraints on people's actions toward one another. It is not the results to be achieved but rather the way people interact with one another that is the proper subject matter of a theory of distributive justice.

Broadly, people ought not to act toward one another in ways that compromise the autonomy of those others. People should be allowed to exercise their full range of choice. This implies that the means of all interaction between people should be voluntary. To force someone to do something, except in cases of retributive justice where that person has herself engaged in coercion, is a violation of autonomy, a violation of Kantian side-constraints. Taken to its proper conclusion, this line of thinking requires that the fundamental principle of distributive justice is voluntary interaction, or what Nozick calls *voluntary transfer*.[19]

Nozick defends this idea with a well-known example he constructs concerning the basketball player Wilt Chamberlain. Suppose that, during the heyday of his career, Chamberlain were to come to an agreement with his team owners that, in addition to his salary (which will be the same as all the other players), he will receive 25 cents from every ticket purchased. The owners agree to this; after all, Chamberlain's presence increases attendance for them. The fans are happy with the arrangement, and signal this happiness by voluntarily buying tickets when he plays. Assume further, for the sake of simplicity, that at the beginning of the season everyone – players, owners, fans – starts off with the same amount of money, as in a game of Monopoly. Allow the season to play itself out, and what happens? There is a rearrangement of the distribution of money. Chamberlain is much richer, his fellow players about even, and the fans a bit poorer.

The question Nozick raises is whether this new distribution is unjust. It is markedly unequal, and perhaps, among the fanatics of Chamberlain's game, it has created some poverty. But is it unjust? Should Chamberlain be required to redistribute any of his earnings? Nozick's claim is that he should not. Everyone who participated in the season did so voluntarily. Nobody was coerced. Therefore, everyone in essence agrees to whatever arrangement would result from their behaviors. "The general point illustrated by the Wilt Chamberlain example . . . is that no end-state principle or distributional patterned principle of justice can be continuously realized without continuous interference with people's lives."[20] To put the point in Nozick's terms, the history of the transfers was just, and so the question of the end-state is irrelevant.

There are a number of questions one might raise here. Are most of our interactions in the economic and political realm as voluntary as they are in sports spectatorship? Is getting and holding on to a job, for instance, a voluntary endeavor or does it involve some form of coercion, even if that coercion isn't by a specifiable other person? Alternatively, what do we do with the children of the participants in this arrangement who will start off in radically different positions given; or rather, it is not simply a matter of that. It is, more importantly, a matter of what we can do.

> We can see the person, in terms of *agency*, recognizing and respecting his or her ability to form goals, commitments, values, etc., and we can also see the person in terms of *well-being*, which too calls for attention. This dichotomy is lost in a model of exclusively self-interested motivation, in which a person's agency must be entirely geared toward his own well-being.[27]

A conception of life that recognizes agency as independently valuable reflects the idea, drawn in part from the writings of the philosopher Bernard Williams,[28] that life is a matter of projects rather than possessions. We should consider human lives not merely as a series of unrelated acts, but as a set of temporally unfolding projects. To become who I might be, while it requires me to have certain things, is not primarily a matter of that having. It is more a matter of "doings and beings." What gives a life its value is bound up with one's ability to sustain friendships and love relationships, construct a meaningful career, develop one's athletic or artistic talents, and other projects that are not simply the sum of discrete moments but threads that are woven together over time into a coherent and meaningful pattern.

Moreover, the doings and beings that people seek are different from one another. People have different visions of a good life. People in the same society will seek to create themselves in divergent ways. Therefore, any adequate conception of social justice will have not only to reflect the idea that it is lives rather than goods that ultimately matter, but also that those lives are not all of one kind, even under the same social conditions.

For Sen, these insights structure how we should conceive of the goods to which people ought to have access. He proposes a four-part division that reflects both the distinction between agency and well-being and a distinction between achievement and freedom. The latter distinction reflects the idea that there is a difference between what a person actually achieves in her projects and the freedom she has to strive after different goals. It is good to be able to achieve what one has set out to do; but it is also good to have the freedom to set out on different paths, even if one doesn't ultimately choose those paths. This captures the diversity of choices people can make. As Sen sums it up, "The two distinctions yield four different concepts of advantage, related to a person: (1) 'well-being achievement', (2) 'agency achievement', (3) 'well-being freedom', (4) 'agency freedom'."[29]

These are the elements that must be taken into account in any political calculus that is to address adequately the needs of human lives. There must be provision for a person's ability to achieve a certain level of well-being, to achieve certain goals (that may or may not have to do with a person's own well-being), as well as to have access to forms of well-being and to goals that one may or may not choose to have or pursue. This is where the concepts of functioning and capability arise. "The capability approach to a person's advantage is concerned with evaluating it in terms of his or her actual ability to achieve various valuable functionings as a part of living."[30] Functionings are defined in terms of what someone can do or be. Sen gives the examples of being in good health, having self-respect, and being socially integrated. These are matters of both well-being and achievement.

Capabilities, while defined in terms of functionings, add to them the concept of freedom. In a more technical formulation, Sen puts the point this way:

> The capability set is a *set* of such functionings *n*-tuples, representing the various alternative combinations of beings and doings any one (combination) of which a person can choose. Capability is thus defined in the *space* of functionings. If a functioning achievement (in the form of an *n*-tuple of functionings) is a *point* in that space, capability is the *set* of such points (representing the alternative functioning *n*-tuples from which one *n*-tuple can be chosen).[31]

We might put the point this way. People cannot do or be everything they would like. They are limited by the finiteness of life and the fact that certain choices exclude others. In addition, they are limited by their social conditions. Certain social conditions might allow access to particular combinations of doings and beings while other social conditions might allow other combinations. A capability set is the combination of doings and beings to which a person has access in a given set of social conditions. It reflects not only what a person is and does, but also what a person can do or be. To put the point in the terms discussed above, a capability set reflects the kinds of life projects, as well as the resources necessary for those projects, that a person might choose. (Sen's reason for utilizing geometrical terms is to make possible a mathematical translation of these concepts for the purposes of economic evaluation, a project he engages in in his more technical writings.)

The concept of a capability set is one Sen appeals to in his analysis of poverty. What is debilitating about poverty is not merely the lack of access to particular goods; it is not simply a matter of material deprivation. More deeply, poverty restricts the kinds of lives people may lead, the types of projects they may choose and embark on. "The case for reorienting poverty analysis from *low incomes* to *insufficient basic capabilities* can be, ultimately, connected with these alternative foundational concerns [i.e. concerns with the importance of freedom to do or be what one chooses]."[32]

What is the distinction between Sen's approach and that of Rawls and Nozick? Sen has enormous respect for Rawls' ground-breaking work. He writes that, "my greatest intellectual debt is to John Rawls. I am led by his reasoning over quite a bit of territory, and even when I go in a different direction . . . that decision is, to a considerable extent, based on an explicit critique of Rawls' theory."[33] Where, then, does he differ? For Sen, Rawls focuses on achievement at the expense of freedom. Rawls' perspective answers to the problem of well-being achievement and agency achievement, but not to the capability sets attaching to these. Contrasting his view with Rawls', Sen writes, "In the capability-based assessment of justice, individual claims are not to be assessed in terms of the resources or primary goods the persons respectively hold, but by the freedoms they actually enjoy to choose the lives that they have reason to value."[34] Because Rawls focuses on what people have or what they deserve to have, he neglects the importance of choosing life's projects (and, because of this, also neglects the different types of lives people often choose) and thus the responsibility of public institutions to provide access to that choice.

Sen does not believe that Rawls' view precludes freedom entirely, but rather that, because it remains focused on resources and goods, on havings rather than doings and beings, it does not achieve the nascent goal it has in view.

> The focus on basic capabilities can be seen as a natural extension of Rawls's concern with primary goods, shifting attention from goods to what goods can do to human beings. Rawls himself motivates judging advantage in terms of primary goods by referring to capabilities, even though his criteria end up focusing on goods as such: on income rather than on what income does, on the "social bases of self-respect" rather than on self-respect itself, and so on.[35]

The shift from having to doing and being has a superficial affinity with Nozick's approach. It emphasizes what people do, what they make of themselves, rather than what they are given. It is not coincidental that both Nozick and Sen center their analyses on the idea of freedom. For both, it is the choosing of our lives that matters rather than what simply the goods to which we have access.

This affinity is, however, no more than superficial. The deeper differences between them emerge when we compare their views of life goals. Nozick's conception of a life, at least insofar as it has relevance to political justice, is fundamentally acquisitive. It is not so much what we make *of* ourselves as what we make *for* ourselves that is at stake in his thought. Consider the Wilt Chamberlain example. It is anchored in the extra cents Chamberlain has contracted for, not in a broader vision of life projects to which he might devote himself. Nozick's entitlement theory does not address the ways Chamberlain might choose to express himself through his talent or, alternatively, ignore his talent for the sake of other projects that perhaps he finds more meaningful. This is one reason for the worry, cited earlier, that Nozick does not address the question of what does and does not constitute voluntary exchange. His concept of freedom is not really a concept of self-creation but instead of self-aggrandizement. Therefore, the question of what kinds of person one can make oneself, what Sen would call one's capability set, does not arise for him. The freedom that interests him is freedom from interference by institutional intervention in pursuing and retaining the goods one desires.

At the structural level, Sen's thought is indeed more closely aligned with that of his claimed predecessor Rawls. He is interested in a form of equal consideration, oriented toward the kinds of lives people choose rather than the kinds of goods and resources to which they can have access. Sen's answer to the question, "Equality of what?" in an essay of the same name is: equality of basic capability. He recognizes that different social conditions preclude everyone from enjoying rich capability sets, and yet wants to provide a marker for equality that does not rely solely on goods, a marker that recognizes that the poor as well as the rich seek to create significant lives, lives that have value to them. Therefore, it should be the goal of social policy to ensure that people have at least the basic ability to create those lives, with both the goods and the freedoms that involves. Of course, the higher the basic level the better; but whatever the level is, it should be a level of capabilities as Sen has defined them: access to various important functionings, matters of doing and being.

It is also here, in the structural affinity with Rawls, that one can see Sen's approach as one of passive rather than active equality. Admittedly, in contrast to Rawls, Sen focuses on what people can do or be, or what they choose to do or be. But their doings and beings do not express or create equality. People do not make and are not responsible for the equality to which they should have access. It is quite the opposite. Bringing about equality of basic capability – indeed, equality of *any* capability – is the responsibility of larger institutions. It is the responsibility of states and larger non-state institutions to ensure that everyone has equal access to the creation of meaningful lives. This does not mean that people cannot themselves have a role to play in creating these conditions. What it does mean is that fundamentally those conditions are owed to them; it is something they can reasonably lay claim to, reasonably expect to have access to, and have a reasonable complaint if not provided to them. It is a matter, to anticipate a term, of people's *rights*.

We saw that from behind the veil of ignorance, people would give equal consideration to every possible position that could be occupied in a society. Sen has no difficulty with this approach. The modification he makes to Rawls' view is in seeking to shift equal consideration from a focus on what resources people have access to toward what kinds of lives they have access to. By introducing the concept of capabilities, Sen inserts into Rawls' broad framework a richer concept of life as one of choices of and engagement in projects. In addition, part of the brilliance of Sen's work is to construct a way of thinking about equality that addresses, both conceptually and mathematically, the problem of poverty without losing sight of the fact that lives, including the lives of the poor, involve projects. The poor are not simply holes to be filled with goods.

Sen conceives of human living as active engagement, and conceives of equality in terms of providing access to that engagement. This remains, however, a form of passive equality. By retaining the central Rawlsian concept of equal consideration, Sen still allots the responsibility for equality to institutions, even while he makes the equality those institutions are responsible for more vibrant and engaged. In short, Sen has a rich conception both of activity and of equality; what he does not have is a conception of active equality. As he taught us at the outset, "a common characteristic of virtually all approaches to the ethics of social arrangements that have stood the test of time is to want equality of *something*." It is in the *wanting* rather than the *creating*, in the desire for it to happen or to have happen *to* one, that the passivity of Sen's equality ultimately lies.

Iris Marion Young, we have seen, wants to jettison what she calls the distributive paradigm. In her view, it focuses too much on material goods, it treats people as static rather than dynamic, evolving beings, it neglects the role that power plays, and it ignores our capacities and ability to participate in the formation of our lives. I would argue that several of Young's criticisms are inapplicable to the framework Sen has constructed. In particular, Sen moves the discussion of distributive justice away from material goods and static lives toward a more dynamic view of capacities. His thought begins, from within the distributive paradigm, to meet some of the criticisms Young brings to bear. He does, however, by focusing on equal consideration, continue to neglect the role participation plays. That role will begin to move us from passive to active equality, and will thus form the bridge to the politics I want to defend here, a politics that is democratic in the deepest sense.

To see Young's criticism, we can return to the distinction, drawn earlier, between oppression and domination. Oppression occurs when people are prevented from adequately learning or expressing their skills and feelings in socially recognized contexts. Oppression is an institutional arrangement that blunts the trajectory of certain lives. Young offers several examples of oppression. Exploitation in the Marxist sense of appropriating the labor of others is a form of oppression. Marginalizing an individual or a social group, rendering people powerless to change their own situation, engaging in "cultural imperialism" where one presents a particular cultural viewpoint as universal, and, of course, committing violence against another are also forms of oppression. Their commonality lies in their creation of a social and political context in which individuals or groups of people are unable to press their own ways of life.

Young is particularly concerned with oppressed groups, and what she often singles out are ways in which the perspectives and forms of life of such groups are stymied by the institutional context in which they take place. African Americans are often exploited, because many of them work in low-paying jobs over which they have little control. They are marginalized by whites through practices like housing discrimination and by the reluctance of many whites to allow their children to date African Americans. They are rendered powerless through relentless critique and a readiness to find them either unqualified or unwilling to fulfill important social roles. African American cultural expression is often considered degenerate and unworthy of serious engagement or study. And violence against African Americans remains common.

Sen, by focusing on capabilities rather than resources, has constructed an approach that goes a long way toward ameliorating oppression. This is unsurprising, since the focus of his work has often been the Third World poor. By attending to the kinds of lives people can create rather than the goods they have access to, his perspective is more sensitive to the institutional problems Young cites. For instance, he could argue that cultural imperialism prevents certain individuals accessing as full a basic equality of capabilities as others. Young's own view is more self-consciously bound to the problem of group oppression than Sen's. However, Sen's approach can be applied to many of the same problems. Furthermore, one might make the argument that it does so without a certain danger that attaches to Young's thought, that of ascribing particular qualities to particular groups in an essentialist way. By focusing on individual choice rather than on group expression, Sen does not run the risk of imposing on particular groups interests or orientations that individual members of those groups may not endorse. He doesn't, for instance, think of a particular form of cultural expression as necessarily "African American."[36]

Sen can address oppression with his perspective. The problem of domination, however, eludes it. Recall Young's definition of domination: "institutional conditions which inhibit or prevent people from participating in determining their actions or the conditions of their actions." Young argues that it is not enough for a just society to possess the conditions for people to live meaningful lives, where they can learn, express, and embrace what is valuable to them without fear of oppression. Justice also involves a participatory component. One must not only be able to carry on one's life but also participate in creating the conditions under which that carrying on is to occur. She tells us, "The values comprised in the good life can be reduced to two very general ones: (1) developing and exercising one's capacities and expressing one's experience . . . and (2) participating in determining one's actions and the conditions of one's action."[37]

A benevolent dictatorship can provide the means necessary for developing one's capacities. It can supply one with what Sen would call broad capability sets. It is not, strictly speaking, necessary for pursuing one's projects that one participate in deciding the institutional arrangements that guarantee the adequate conditions for such a pursuit. In Young's view, such a life would be lacking. Without being able to participate in the conditions under which one constructs one's projects, the worth of those projects is diminished. One's life is impoverished. Participation, alongside the exercise of certain capacities, is necessary for a fully meaningful life.

In Chapter 2 I will argue that, although we need not conceive participation as necessary for the good life, we do need to conceive it as necessary for the formation of democratic politics.

Sen's perspective, as well as Rawls' and Nozick's, cannot accommodate the necessity of participation. It is not that they deny participation as a meaningful activity. None of them has defended the superiority of a benevolent dictatorship. Further, since all of them cite the necessity of institutional structures in order to support their respective distributive proposals, presumably there will be some among those inhabiting their proposed societies who *will* participate in creating the conditions they espouse. Moreover, one might claim that, for Sen at least, a broader capability set would allow access to political participation for those who value it as a project.

The problem is that none of them sees participation as a particularly political good. We found this in particular with Rawls, but it applies equally to Sen and Nozick, and to any distributive theory of justice. Where the issue is distribution rather than participation, even where what is to be distributed are the conditions for an active creation of one's life, there is no internal bond between justice and decision-making.

Young argues that welfare capitalism "constructs citizens as client-consumers, discouraging their active participation in public life . . . the distributive paradigm of justice functions ideologically to reinforce this depoliticization."[38] Her claim here is twofold. First, welfare capitalism has a particular political view of the citizen, a view that sees citizens not as participants in a common political culture or project but as consumers to be satisfied by meeting their individual needs. Welfare capitalism reduces the political to the economic and the economic to the consumerist. Second, distributive theories of justice reinforce this view by focusing discussions of justice on those needs rather than on political participation. When justice is solely a matter of what people are entitled to from the powers that be, then the question of who participates in the powers that be becomes irrelevant.

What Young proposes here, in terms that she does not use but we will, is a form of active equality. This may seem odd, since she does not use the term *equality*, but *participation*. As she uses the latter, however, she implies the former. To stake out a claim for participation is at the same time to claim one's ability to participate, to press the idea that one is no less qualified in deciding the conditions of one's political existence than those who have decided those conditions until

41. "On the Jewish Question," in Karl Marx, *Early Writings*. tr. Rodney Livingston and Gregor Benton. New York: Vintage, 1975, p. 230.
42. Claude Lefort, "Politics and Human Rights," tr. Alan Sheridan, in Claude Lefort, *The Political Forms of Modern Society*, ed. John B. Thompson. Cambridge, MA: MIT Press, 1986 (essay or. pub. 1980), p. 261.

CHAPTER 2

Active Equality: Democratic Politics

In the early morning of May 12, 2001, a young African American, Kashef White, was hit by a car and killed in my home town of Clemson, South Carolina. A white male student at Clemson University was the car's driver. There are very few facts about what happened that night that are not in dispute. Witnesses at the scene, which was outside a small club, said that the Kashef had one foot on the sidewalk and one in the street; the driver veered toward the curb and hit Kashef, unintentionally but negligently. The driver and the police said that Kashef had been in the middle of the road. The witnesses said that the car was driving at breakneck speed. The police and the driver denied this. Witnesses said that it took police upward of twenty-five minutes to reach the scene, by which time Kashef was dead. Police argued that they arrived several minutes after they were called. It should perhaps be noted that the witnesses were all African American, the police white.

Among the undisputed facts are these: the police smelled alcohol on the driver's breath and gave him a field sobriety test but not a blood alcohol test; they did, however, perform a blood alcohol test on the dead African American, and found him to have been intoxicated. The driver's uncle, a former sheriff in Greenville, South Carolina, subsequently referred to the deceased as a "drunk black kid."

A week after Kashef's death, nearly a quarter of Clemson's black community attended a meeting with the chief of police and other officers and confronted them with a litany of both city and police neglect and abuse. The range of accusations was as broad as it was unsurprising, from police abuses like stopping people for driving while black to bribery to city neglect of roads and parks in African American neighborhoods. It was unclear to me, as I sat in the meeting, which among the accusations was true and how much was exaggeration. What was clear was that at least some of it was true and that the African American community had been scarred by it.

I later learned that one of the defining incidents for Clemson's small African American community had been a beating, thirty years earlier, of an outspoken African American male while in police custody. The beating was so violent that it left the man mentally incapacitated. One can still see him wandering the streets of the African American neighborhoods on daily but purposeless meanderings. No policeman was ever charged with the beating, and several of those said to be involved now hold prominent positions in the police department in Clemson and a neighboring town.

In the wake of the meeting following Kashef's death, I worked as a community organizer with Clemson's African American community for two years. Our ostensible goal was to seek redress for police conduct on the night of May 12 and to create a civilian review board to oversee police abuse. Beyond that, though, we were trying to create a sense of unity and purpose among the very disorganized African American community in Clemson, a community whose attitudes toward itself and toward the white community was little different from what one would have expected to find in the 1950s. We went door to door on numerous occasions, talking to residents about their experiences and educating them about community organizing. We held planning meetings that, for the first six months or so, were well attended. Eventually, we ran two candidates from the African American community for the City Council. They lost, but one of them made it to a runoff vote.

For its part, the city engaged in a variety of small measures designed both to address certain African American concerns and to forestall the momentum of any organizing effort. Videotape machines were installed in police cars. Roads that had been neglected for years were finally paved. Housing repairs were made. Several scholarships were offered to local African American youths to the local rec center. And, of course, there was the inevitable task force that met for several years to address concerns about a racism that was officially denied by the mayor and the City Council.

The events that I am describing here are not uncommon. In fact, they are depressing in their familiarity. Everyone knows of incidents like these. The question I want to raise here is one of how to understand what happened. How might we think about the events that followed the death of Kashef White? What do we make of the organizing efforts and the city's reaction?

One way to approach these events might be to deny the existence of any interesting threads that run through them. This would be the approach of what we might call the radical empiricist. Someone was killed, it might be said. It was an accident. The police may or may not have arrived on time, and while their performing a blood alcohol test on the victim was perhaps unfortunate, there is nothing to be learned from this. People organized in the community because there was anger there and because there was an organizer. The city tried to help in ways that cities often try to help, sincerely but inadequately. There you have it.

Although the City Council of Clemson employs no philosophers, it was consistently wedded to this radically empiricist approach.

We will not embrace this approach. We must turn elsewhere. My suggestion is that we turn to the thought of a recent French historian and theorist, Jacques Rancière. By pursuing several elements of his political theoretical framework, we can understand better not only what happened in Clemson over the course of the years that followed Kashef's death, but also how a politics of active equality, a truly democratic politics, is to work.

Perhaps the best way to start is with the concept of politics itself. For Rancière, politics is not a common occurrence. "[P]olitics doesn't always happen," he writes. "[I]t happens very little or rarely."[1] This does not mean, of course, that politics as we understand it in the everyday sense is a rare event. People vote; they write to their elected representatives; sometimes they join a demonstration. Politics as a matter of passive equality is common. And, in fact, as we will discuss in Chapter 5, politics in the everyday sense may be inescapable.

For Rancière, however, voting, writing to elected representatives, even attending a demonstration, are not by themselves matters of politics. Politics concerns something else: it concerns equality. And equality arises only when the traditional mechanisms of what are usually called "politics" are put into question. "Politics only occurs," he tells us, "when these mechanisms are stopped in their tracks by the effect of a presupposition that is totally foreign to them yet without which none of them could ultimately function: the presupposition of the equality of anyone and everyone."[2]

Politics concerns the presupposition of equality. This seems to be an obvious truth, an uncontroversial place to start political thought. We saw this in Chapter 1. Rancière, however, is not thinking about the presupposition of equality in any of the ways that have come down to us through our history. He reworks the presupposition, and in reworking it, changes its inflection from passive to active.

In Chapter 1, we discussed passive equality and its relation to theories of distributive justice. For Rancière, passive equality is not politics; it is policing. "What generally goes by the name of politics is the set of procedures whereby the aggregation and consent of collectivities is achieved, the organization of powers, the distribution of places and roles, and the systems for legitimizing this distribution. I propose to give this system of distribution and legitimization another name. I propose to call it the *police*."[3] Before deepening the concept of politics, of what we will call *democratic politics* (in order both to distinguish it from the mainstream politics of passive equality and, inextricably, to emphasize that it is a politics of the *demos*, the people) we will start with the character of policing, since we have already seen it in the previous chapter.

Although Rancière does not discuss the distributive theorists of mainstream Anglo-American political philosophy, his definition of policing is an exact depiction of the goals of such philosophy. The question animating these theories is one of how to distribute the social goods or the conditions under which people can exercise their lives. We have not used the term policing, since we tend to associate it with uniformed people keeping order. However, there is another association one might make with the term, an association more accurate to the term's origin. This association is with the a set of lectures by Michel Foucault in the late 1970s, where he discusses the origin of the term *policing* in the seventeenth century. As Foucault points out, policing did not originally refer to anything particularly military. Rather, policing involved a broader set of practices concerned to do with the health of the state.

The police as Foucault discovers it concerns the regulation of and concern for the health and productivity of the lives of a state's citizens. It occupies a position that is not one of law, but of ensuring a population's well-being in order that a state may thrive. The police is a matter of what Foucault calls "governmentality," the practice of governing. "The police is governmentality directed by the sovereign insofar as he is sovereign."[4] The role of the police, then, is to ensure, for the sake of the sovereign and the state, a smoothly functioning population. Foucault says of the German theorist Von Justi,

> he defines much more clearly what the central paradox of *police* is. The police, he says, is what enables the state to increase its power and to exert its strength to the full. On the other hand, the police has to keep the citizens happy – happiness being understood as survival, life, and improved living. He perfectly defines what I feel to be the aim of the modern art of government, or state rationality: viz., to develop those elements constitutive of individuals' lives in such a way that their development also fosters that of the strength of the state.[5]

Rancière's use of the term police is not exactly the same as Foucault's. It is not concerned solely with practices of governmentality, and it is not embedded in a view of politics that was prevalent in the seventeenth and eighteenth centuries. However, like Foucault's treatment, Rancière's use of the term keeps alive the idea of the police as involving a social ordering that is enforced not merely by military-style intervention – armed men in uniforms – but more significantly by the idea of a proper social order.

Policing, as Rancière defines it, is deeply embedded in Western political philosophy. Rancière himself locates the first instance of it in Plato's *Republic*. Recall that, for Socrates, people are best fitted for one of three positions in the ideal city, the *kallipolis*, depending on which part of their soul is dominant. For those who are dominated by their appetitive or acquisitive part, the best role they can play is that of merchants and producers. Those who are dominated by their spirit are the guardians of the city. And those who are dominated by reason, who are able to grasp the nature of the forms, and especially that of the Good itself, are to be the rulers. A harmony in the *kallipolis*, corresponding to the harmony of the soul, arises when each part fulfills his or her proper role in the city. Disharmony begins when one tries to occupy a position for which one is not suited. As Socrates explains to Glaucon, "when someone, who is by nature a craftsman or some other kind of money-maker, is puffed up by wealth, or by having a majority of votes, or by his own strength, or by some other such thing, at attempts to enter the class of soldiers . . . then I think you'll agree that these exchanges and this sort of meddling bring the city to ruin."[6]

This tripartite division of the city is reflected in the myth – the falsehood, as Socrates acknowledges – of the three metals: gold, silver, and bronze. " 'All of you in the city are brothers,' we'll say to them in telling our story, 'but the god who made you mixed some gold into those who are adequately equipped to rule, because they are the most valuable. He put silver in those who are auxiliaries and iron and bronze in the farmers and craftsmen.' "[7] The story, and the *kallipolis* it is to support, display both passive equality and inequality, and indeed show the former to be a matter of the latter. For Socrates, a good city is a harmonious one. Everyone is better off in a harmonious city. In order for harmony to reign, however, there are some who must decide how the city is to be ruled, and others who are to be ruled. In this sense, although everyone is equal – in that everyone has a contribution to make to the health of the city – the particular role of some is to be decided by others. The money-makers and the auxiliary guardians are to receive the particular equality that is arranged by the rulers.

However, as Socrates makes clear, this is not simply a matter of passive equality. Those whose natures are mixed with gold are "the most valuable." They are more important for the city than the others. They are not more important in the sense that the city can exist without them; the city requires everyone in order to exist and to flourish. They are more important in that they possess the most valuable skills, the skills associated with understanding harmony and not merely contributing to it.

One might ask here what it is that makes that skill, which is only one among others necessary for the harmonious flourishing of the city, more valuable than other skills. It is unclear whether Socrates, or Plato, would have an adequate answer that does not already presuppose the "higher" nature of such a skill. However, at issue here is not the justifiability of this presupposition, but merely its existence. Those who decide the character of the city, while in one sense equal to others in the city, are, we might say, more equal than others.

Rancière inaugurates the term "archipolitics" as a description of Plato's approach to politics. "Archipolitics, whose model is supplied by Plato, reveals in all its radicality the project of a community founded on the integral realization, the integral sensibility of the *arkhê* of the community, ceaselessly replacing the democratic configuration of politics."[8] In archipolitics, everything has its place. Harmony reigns. There is no politics, because there is no assertion of equality. Politics is eliminated because, rather than anyone acting out of the presupposition of equality, everyone is allotted a proper place and is expected to remain there. Policing replaces politics as the project of a political philosophy.

In the end, the goal of policing is precisely that of eliminating politics, democratic politics. The existence of democratic politics, we will see, is disruptive of order, particularly of any order that allots people to places or, alternatively, allots places for people to fill. The expression of equality brings disharmony; it is an act of dissensus from a current social order. Therefore, democratic politics is directly opposed to policing. Inversely, the project of policing, which Rancière thinks is the project of much of the history of political philosophy, is that of suppressing or keeping at bay a democratic politics.

Archipolitics is not the only form of policing in the history of political philosophy. Rancière cites two others, both more recent in origin:

parapolitics and metapolitics. Parapolitics finds it origin in Aristotle, who, more nearly democratic than Plato, is not content to shunt equality aside so peremptorily. "No doubt," says Aristotle, "it would be better if the most virtuous were to rule over the city and if they were to rule forever. But this natural order of things is impossible wherever you have a city where 'all are by nature equal.' "[9] There is a tension in Aristotle's thought between quality on the one hand and equality on the other. Aristotle's solution is to have each form of government go against its natural tendency, in order to incorporate its competing principle. Tyrants or oligarchs must act for the betterment of the people, thus introducing good government on the one hand and maintaining the veneer of equality on the other. "[P]olitics is a question of aesthetics, a matter of appearances. The good regime is one that takes on the appearances of an oligarchy for the oligarchs and democracy for the demos."[10]

Rancière notes that the tradition of parapolitics is continued in Thomas Hobbes, who places the Aristotelian tension in individuals rather than the state: individuals must alienate their natural bent toward freedom in order to create and sustain a proper state. Indeed, the liberal tradition of contractarianism, stemming from the idea that individuals possess a natural equality that is then subordinated to a particular state order, is parapolitical. It is not just in ancient Greece, then, that parapolitics stakes its political claims. Any theory that seeks to recognize equality within a more general order of policing is a form of parapolitics.

Parapolitics, while recognizing equality in a more straightforward way than archipolitics, remains rooted in the idea of the police. Its goal is to eliminate expressions of equality. Instead of people's acting out of the presupposition of their equality with those who rule, the latter must give expression to the desires of the former. If there is an equality here, and in many cases there is one, it remains a passive equality. It is an equality that is distributed to rather than created by those who are its object.

Metapolitics is a particularly modern phenomenon whose exemplar is Karl Marx. For metapolitics, politics itself, the very idea of politics, is a gloss for injustices that are happening elsewhere. For metapolitics, the truth of politics lies elsewhere, outside or beyond politics (thus *meta*politics) and, conversely, politics is the falsifier of the truth. "In the modern 'political philosophy' apparatus, the truth of politics is no longer located above politics as its essence or idea. It is located beneath or behind it, in what it conceals and exists only to conceal."[11]

In order to grasp this, consider a simplified version of Marxist doctrine. The real relations between human beings are determined not by the political order but by the economic one. There are those who exploit and those who are exploited. The political relations among people serve simply to conceal this fact. How does this concealment work? Through the ideology of individualism and human rights. The nominally democratic state allows each individual to express his or her views through voting and it protects each individual's basic freedoms. The state, in other words, appears as the institution through which justice is preserved. In particular, the state protects the rights of individuals to enter freely into contracts with one another. This appearance of the preservation of justice serves only to conceal the fact that those "freely" entered into contracts are mechanisms for class exploitation. If we seek to understand how a society is operating, then, we must turn away from the level of politics and concentrate on that of economics. In short, the truth of the political – justice – is to be found elsewhere; politics is solely a concealment of that truth.

Marxism is not the only form of metapolitics. Rancière points out that the European neoliberalism of the 1990s, which to all appearances would seem the opposite of Marxism, is in fact a form of metapolitics. Neoliberalism is bound to the idea of "the end of politics," that the economic will attend to the needs formerly pressed in the political sphere. In this sense, ironically, "The 'end of politics' is the ultimate phase of metapolitical interference, the final affirmation of the emptiness of its truth. The 'end of politics' is the completion of political philosophy."[12]

All of these forms of policing blunt the force of a democratic politics.[13] That is their point: to prevent the active expression of equality by those who are not in charge of their political lives. "[W]hat is called 'political philosophy' might well be the set of reflective operations whereby philosophy tries to have done with politics."[14] Rancière refers to those who do not participate in the decisions that order their political lives, the demos, as "the part that has no part" (*le part sans-part*). The goal of political philosophy is to create or foster or militate for a police order to ensure that the part that has no part continues to have no part. Political philosophy justifies their having no part. To be sure, this happens in different ways in the three forms of political philosophy. Archipolitics allots unequal places for each in the name of the common good; parapolitics blunts the force of the assumption of equality by seeking to create an order that requires compromising it; metapolitics abandons the field of political struggle for equality altogether in the name of a non-political element. But they converge on the point of ensuring that the part that has no part continues to have no part. (This claim may seem strange when applied to Marxism. However, Marxism's embrace of an avantgarde party makes it seem less so. We will return to this idea in more depth in Chapter 3.)

Where do the political philosophies of Chapter 1 fall? Rawls, Nozick, and Sen in particular offer exercises in parapolitics. Unlike Plato, they are committed to equality. Unlike Marx and the proponents of the end of politics, they believe that politics has its own integrity. It is not simply a mask for something else. (Although for Nozick that integrity is a thin one, involving a minimal state. In that sense, his thought is closer to the metapolitics of neoliberalism, while still leaving a role for the state in ensuring that side constraints are protected.) What each asks of the *demos*, of the people who are its object, is that they ratify an order that distributes the social goods or the conditions for obtaining or realizing those goods without necessarily participating in that distribution. Each offers an equality whose price is to be its recipient rather than its creator. Each, in its own way, embraces the concept of equality while requiring the realization of that equality to turn its subject into an object. That is the tradeoff of parapolitics: to recognize equality while allowing the best to govern. And that is why Iris Young has one foot in parapolitics and one foot outside. She sees the necessity of participation in equality, but then requires for its realization an order that is outside its expression, a police order.

To think of politics in terms of policing is our common approach. Its province lies not only among political philosophers. Those of us on the left often ask ourselves questions like the following: What degree of health care is everyone entitled to? What should the legally enforced minimum wage be? Should the construction of voting districts reflect the racial distribution of populations? During the heyday of identity politics, demands were often issued on the basis of what was owed to African Americans or women or gays and lesbians. These are not questions of how the demos should be, but of what it should receive, what it is entitled to. They are questions of distribution.

There is nothing wrong with these questions as far as they go. They are not, however, at least on their own, a matter of politics as Rancière conceives it. Politics, what I am beginning to call here *democratic politics*, is not a matter of how distributions occur. Distributions are what governments do. But they are not what people do – the people who should be the subject of politics. At the heart of questions and theories of distributions lies a certain passivity. Distributions happen to people; people do not make them happen. Or, if people make them happen, it is only indirectly, by making others make them happen.

Suppose we were to reverse the procedure. Suppose that, instead of putting equality at the end of the process, we were to put it at the beginning. Suppose that we were to treat equality not as a debt, not as a matter of obligatory distribution, but as what Rancière has called a *presupposition*. Democratic politics concerns the presupposition of equality, not its distribution. What would it mean to put equality at the beginning of a political process rather than at the end of a police process? How would it work? How might we conceive it?

We can approach this question from two directions. One way would be through negation, to ask how a democratic politics intervenes upon and interferes with a police order. What does politics stop from happening? The other way would be through a positive direction, asking instead what a democratic politics creates, what it expresses, and what it makes happen.

We start with the negative direction. Rancière characterizes politics as a dissensus. When people act out of the presupposition of equality, they engage in a dissensus from the police order that has acted to deny their equality. "The essence of politics is a *dissensus*," he writes, explaining that,[15] "Dissensus is not the confrontation between interests or opinions. It is the manifestation of a distance of the sensible from itself." This explanation becomes clearer when we pose it next to Rancière's claim that, "Politics is specifically opposed to the police. The police is a 'partition of the sensible' [*le partage du sensible*] whose principle is the absence of a void or a supplement."[16] What a police order seeks is to put everything in its place, through allotment and through justification. The allotment is the distribution posited by the order. The justification, at least in its contemporary form, is the appeal to equality that founds the particular distribution.

As we have seen, however, the equalities of a police order, when they exist, are at best passive. They are distributions to people rather than expressions by them. In that sense, they presuppose at least one inequality: between those who distribute and those who receive the distribution. This is not an insignificant inequality. It concerns more than the fact of distribution. It concerns the character of empowerment. There are those who are in charge of allotments and those who are not, those who make decisions and those for whom they are made. Traditional political philosophy, because it is concerned with the justice of the distributions themselves rather than the question of participation, obscures this distinction. This has two other effects: it excludes the recipients from political involvement and covers up that exclusion with illusions of wholeness or completeness. That is what Rancière means by "the absence of a void or a supplement": that the demos are made to disappear and that their disappearance is itself hidden by the police order.

We have already seen this exclusion at work. In distributive theories of justice, people do not participate in the creation of their political lives. Or, more precisely, their participation, if it happens, is not integral to political justice. As Rawls has told us, when the decision about the principles of justice are made, people "return to their place in society." They do not, at least as people of the polity, participate in the shaping of the social order. They have no part. It is the elites, those who *represent* the people, rather than the people themselves, who have a part.

This is not all. These theories render this exclusion invisible. By justifying a police order through meeting the criterion of equality, this inequality of participation is effaced. It is as though, once everything has its place, it becomes impossible, or nearly so, to see the inequalities that have been created. This is why Rancière uses the term "sensible." It is not just that places or roles have been partitioned. The partitioning concerns an entire experience. We experience a whole divided into its proper parts, each allotted its proper place, with no remainder. Foucault emphasizes how people are created and molded to experience the world in ways that are ultimately oppressive to them. Rancière's idea of a partition of the sensible circulates in the same arena as Foucault's historical analyses. It concerns the ways in which who we might be, how we might create our own political lives, are hidden from us by our experience of the world. The specific experience he is concerned with, however, is that of politics and the justification of particular police orders.

If a police order is characterized by a partition of the sensible that renders invisible the part that has no part, then a democratic politics is, as Rancière tells us, "the manifestation of a distance of the sensible from itself." A partition of the sensible in the police order covers over the void or supplement that is partly constitutive of it. There is no police order without the participation of the people, those people who are politically invisible, each in her proper place. There is something in the sensible, then, that can, by expressing itself, disrupt the sensible that it partially constitutes. When that something does in fact express itself, it manifests the internal disruption of the sensible, the distance of the sensible from itself. A democratic politics occurs when that manifestation happens. This does not mean that the disruption, the manifestation, is always there. In this sense, Rancière's thought is distinct from the deconstruction of Jacques Derrida, whose deconstructive structure of the play of presence and absence it resembles at this point. "[P]olitics doesn't always happen . . . it happens very little or rarely." But happen it does.

And when it does, it does so as a dissensus from the police order, a manifestation of the distance of the sensible from itself. Why is this manifestation not "a confrontation between interests and opinions"? It is because it is an action by the people, the demos, that intervenes upon the situation. The demos has been excluded. A democratic politics is the appearance of that which has been excluded. This is an intervention, not a discussion. "This is precisely why politics cannot be identified with the model of communicative action [i.e. the thought of Habermas] since this model presupposes the partners in communicative exchange to be pre-constituted, and that the discursive forms of exchange imply a speech community whose constraint is always explicable."[17] Democratic politics manifests a people. In a sense we will discuss below, it creates a political subject. It is not a conversation among subjects who have already been established in their character. After all, if one is invisible, what character can one have?

In this way, democratic politics is a dissensus, a dissensus from a police order that marginalizes and excludes. In the name of equality (an equality that will be explicated when we turn to the positive character of democratic politics), a demos arises that dissents from the position or positions its members have been allotted. A people disrupts the completeness of a police order through an activity that is in itself an expression of its own equality with those whose own position or actions seek to deny that equality.

Because it is a dissensus, democratic politics has another negative feature, that of declassification. "The essence of equality is not so much to unify as to declassify, to undo the supposed naturalness of orders and replace it with the controversial figures of division."[18] The project of a democratic politics, a politics of equality, is to reject the marginalized position to which one has been assigned, not for the sake of another or different position, but for the sake of nothing at all other than one's own equality.

In order to grasp this idea we must be careful, because it is easy to misread Rancière. There is no specific group of people who are the demos, the part that has no part, as though it were those people and no others. In a police order, there are many types of classifications that create many types of inequality. There are economic classifications, racial and gender classifications, psychological and sociological classifications. This approach is distinct from that of Marx, for whom the working class is the particular object of exploitation and therefore the subject of political action. For Rancière, the people, the demos, consists of those who, in a given classification, are unequal to others in that classification. They can be women, gays, African Americans, *sans papiers*, students, *mestizos*, Tibetans, workers, etc. The people are those who have no claim to contribute to the public discussion and debate, those who are, from the perspective of the police order – or some aspect of that order – invisible. Politics, then, is a process of declassification. It is a process of abandoning the identity one has been given. To substitute another identity for the previous one would be simply to construct another police order. The movement of declassification, then, is not preliminary to another movement of reclassification. It is a purely negative moment in the politics of equality.

Consider the following example.

> Monday, February 1 [1960], students at the Negro colleges around Greensboro, North Carolina, were electrified by reports of what four freshmen boys had done that day . . . the four of them had gone to the downtown Woolworth's and slipped into seats at the sacrosanct whites-only lunch counter . . . Because the four students at Woolworth's had no plan, they began with no self-imposed limitations. They defined no tactical goals. They did not train or drill in preparation. They did not dwell on the many forces that might be used against them. Above all, they did not anticipate that Woolworth's white managers would – instead of threatening to have them arrested – flounder in confusion and embarrassment.[19]

The first lunch counter sit-in was simple. Four people sat down at the lunch counter of Woolworth's with the goal of ordering lunch. Of course they were not served. Their orders were not taken. In fact, the African American waitress behind the counter berated them for their provocation. How might we characterize this protest? There seems to be no better way than to see it as an expression of equality that is at once a dissensus and a declassification. As an expression of equality, the four African American students were doing nothing other than engaging in an activity that whites took for granted. They did not ask for equal treatment. They did not call upon the government to distribute to them the means of living equally with whites. Instead, they *presupposed* their own equality to whites and acted out of that presupposition. That they had no particular plan, that the sit-in was spontaneous, was not necessary to its being an expression of equality. On the other hand, it does indicate a certain "naturalness" to the action, an assumption of equality that was taken for granted among them.

To act in this way, at this time, to presuppose one's equality as an African American, was, of course, a dissensus from the police order. In that order, African Americans were allotted a place that made them clearly unequal to whites. The educational doctrine of the time known as "separate but equal" was, as everyone knew, indeed separate but anything but equal. Separate would not be equal. It never was and is not now. To seek to integrate through the expression of equality was an act of dissent from that police order. This much is obvious.

What is less obvious is that this dissent was also a form of declassification. The four students who sat down at the lunch counter, and the many that followed them, were not seeking a new classification. They did not want to be white. They did not want to be treated as white or to occupy the position allotted to whites. What they were struggling against was the very division into whites and Negroes. They did not want to substitute another classification in the place of this one. They simply wanted to destroy the classifications that were ordering their lives. To be equal without regard to categories is to render those categories irrelevant. This is the precise nature of the presupposition of equality that Rancière finds at the source of any democratic politics.

One might object here, however, that there is more going on than simply a presupposition of equality. There is also a demand: to be treated equally to whites. In fact, it might be said, isn't the demand for equal treatment the more important element here? I have, following Rancière, placed the accent on the behavior of the protesters as an expression of equality. But isn't that the wrong place for the accent? Shouldn't it be placed rather on the demand for equal treatment? And if so, doesn't this return us to the framework of distributive justice? Isn't the issue really one of being treated equally, if not by the governing institutions, then, in this case at least, by the culinary ones?

There is a demand associated with this particular action, and with most democratic action. In Chapter 5 I will argue, against Rancière, that a democratic politics does not need to have a demand associated with it. It is not necessarily agonistic. However, most democratic political action does, and perhaps all democratic action will. While agonism is not a necessary condition of a democratic politics, it may be that, empirically, that's how it always turns out. The question we face here is whether this demand returns us to the passive equality of the theories canvassed in the previous chapter.

It does not. In the lunch counter sit-in, what created the demand was the action itself, the presupposition of equality that was expressed in the behavior of sitting down at the lunch counter with the intention of ordering a meal. Contrast this with Rawls' or Sen's view. An individual in a society operating in accordance with their theories can reasonably expect to receive the goods, both material and immaterial (like rights), that are a foundation for constructing a meaningful life. They might define those lives differently, especially with regard to the issue of freedom, but the idea of reasonable expectation remains. In Nozick's view, they can expect to receive nothing of that sort, but they do expect not to be interfered with by others in the construction of a life, and particularly in the acquisitions they make. If these reasonable expectations are not met, then there is a political problem. People might ask of the governing institutions that they meet their stated obligations, or they might demonstrate, or, if the governing institution proves unyielding, they might vote in a different set of people to govern. In other words, they might act.

What their acting means is that there has been a failure of politics. Politics has not achieved its task, and so corrective action must be taken. This is exactly the opposite of Rancière's view. For him, action does not signify that there has been a failure of politics. Action is the very nature of politics. For theories of distributive justice, the democracy lies in the equality that the members of a society receive or are protected in. Those members are forced to act when that equality does not arise or veers off its path. For Rancière, the democracy lies in the action itself. Democratic politics lies in what one does rather than in what one receives or is entitled to.

This does not mean that there is no demand associated with a democratic politics. Democratic action is often demanding. At times the demands are met, and at times not. Rancière claims that, "a verification [of equality] becomes 'social', causes equality to have a real social effect, only when it mobilizes an *obligation* to hear."[20] This may be going too far; after all, action can be empowering for people even when it fails to mobilize such an obligation. There can be "real social effects" on those who act, solely by virtue of their coming to recognize themselves as actors rather than objects or recipients. Nevertheless, Rancière rightly distinguishes between democratic action and the consequences of that action. A democratic politics is a type of action. It is a collective action that starts from the presupposition of equality. It is, then, in contrast to mainstream political philosophy, a form of active rather than passive equality.

The lunch counter sit-ins were examples of democratic politics because the people participating in them acted out of the presupposition of their equality with whites. True, they may be read, in a sense, as making demands, even if those demands were implicit in their action. But the democratic character of their action lay not in the demands themselves but in the action they took. That action was both a form of dissensus and of declassification, a dissensus and a declassification that were intrinsic to the action itself rather than attached to it from the outside. The very act of an African American sitting down at a lunch counter is a dissensus from the police order that says that blacks cannot sit down at places normally occupied by whites. And by that fact, it is a declassification of the distinction between African Americans and whites.

It may be that the lunch counter sit-ins are a particularly apt example of Rancièrian politics. But how widely might democratic politics cast its net? Can we say, for instance, that strikes or demonstrations are instances of democratic politics? Let us look at strikes, and then at demonstrations. Workers walk off a job, demanding higher wages. Does this not constitute a form of traditional politics? Can we really say in this case that the workers are acting out of the presupposition of equality? In the lunch counter sit-ins, the equality was directly acted: people sat down to order lunch, just like whites. With a strike, however, it would be odd to say that one walks off the job, just like the bosses. Wouldn't it be more accurate to say that a strike indicates a failure of politics, a failure of just distributions, than to call it a moment of active equality?

Rancière offers us a case study of a strike as an example of democratic politics. In 1830, the French adopted a Charter that declares that all French people are equal before the law. In 1833, French tailors went out on strike, demanding higher wages and better working conditions. One of the heads of the bosses, a Monsieur Schwartz, responded to the strike by forming a federation of bosses. Under French law, both the tailors' federation and the bosses' federation were illegal. However, only the tailors' federation was prosecuted. Rancière puts this situation in the form of a syllogism. "The syllogism is simple: the major premiss contains what the law has to say; the minor, what is said or done elsewhere, any word or deed which contradicts the fundamental legal/political affirmation of equality."[21]

There is an internal tension in this syllogism. The minor premise contradicts the major one. The major premise affirms equality in words, the minor one contradicts it in action. What the strike accomplishes is to force this contradiction out into the open. As Rancière puts it, "If Monsier Persil [the prosecutor] or Monsieur Schwartz is right to say what he says and do what he does, the preamble of the Charter must be deleted. It should read: the French people are not equal. If, by contrast, the major premiss is upheld, then Monsieur Persil or Monsieur Schwartz must speak or act differently."[22]

Of course, the French were not prepared to amend the Charter. The Charter reflected a deep sense of French normative commitments (a point we will return to in Chapter 4). The first alternative Rancière cites is offered ironically. The strike, then, presses the boss and the prosecutor to act differently. It is a demand for equality. But does this not return us to the question we raised earlier? Is a strike like this nothing more than a traditional form of passive equality?

We can begin to see here why it is not. The demand for equality arises, as it did in the lunch counter sit-ins, on the basis of an action. That action – the strike – is made because of the tailors' presupposition of their equality. It was not that the tailors wondered whether they were equal or not, and went on strike to find out whether they should be treated as equals; or whether, alternatively, the preamble to the Charter should be changed. They presupposed their own equality and therefore went on strike. The strike was an action expressive of their sense of equality. They did not, as the lunch counter protesters did, act like those they were presupposing their equality to. They could not; that was not a course of action that was open to them. Rather, they expressed their equality in the way they could: by utilizing their collective power as workers in order to force a social recognition of what they already presupposed.

This does not mean that every strike must arise out of the presupposition of equality. For instance, a strike by workers who oppose the hiring of immigrants would hardly be an expression of equality; it would be an expression of superiority. One might even take issue with Rancière's example, arguing that the issue at stake there was not equality, but wages and working conditions. There are two responses to be given here. The first is more theoretical. Whether or not this particular strike was an expression of equality, Rancière has shown in his analysis how it can be that a strike is such an expression. One can engage in a politics of demand that is also a democratic politics. There is no necessary contradiction between active equality and a demand to be recognized as equal. The second response is closer to the case. It would seem that most strikes for higher wages and better working conditions contain at least an element of active equality. Because they arise from a sense that those who work deserve to be treated in a more nearly equal way to those who employ them, there is an orientation of such strikes toward the presupposition of equality, even when they are not explicitly or deeply implicitly tied to that presupposition.

If strikes can be forms of democratic politics, what about demonstrations? Let us take, for example, a demonstration in solidarity with a political movement occurring in another country. If people in the United States demonstrate in solidarity with the Zapatistas in Chiapas or the Tibetans, in what sense are they expressing equality? They are certainly not doing what the tailors were doing in France: expressing their own equality in the face of those who would deny it. How should we think of cases like this?

Demonstrations like these are expressions that unify those who are oppressed and those who act alongside them and on their behalf into a single subject. We will discuss the political process of subjectification below as the outcome of a democratic politics. For now, we can say that what happens in a demonstration is the formation of a subject of politics that aligns a portion of those who have a part with those who do not. The essential message of a solidarity movement is not, "We are equal to those who oppress us." It is, "We stand alongside those who are oppressed, as equals, in the creation of a single political subject." Those who participate in a solidarity movement are not among the part that has no part. They are men who demonstrate for women's rights, straights who demonstrate on behalf of gays, Americans and Europeans who stand with the Palestinians, North Americans who oppose exploitation of South America, people who support the struggle of the Zapatistas and the indigenous populations of Mexico. Together with those who struggle, they form an expression of equality that is further evidence of how a democratic politics is declassifying as well as dissenting. "When the dissidents of the Eastern bloc adopted the term 'hooligans' with which they were stigmatized by the heads of these regimes, when demonstrators in the Paris of 1968 declared, against all police evidence, 'We are all German Jews,' they exposed for all to see the gap between political subjectification . . . and any kind of identification."[23]

We must be clear here. In a police order, there are those who have a part (men, straights, Israelis, etc.), and those who have no part (women, gays, Palestinians, etc.). For a member identified by the police order as someone who has a part to engage in solidarity with those who do not is to participate in the declassification characteristic of a democratic politics. It is *not* to claim that one is the object of a particular inequality, but rather that one is unwilling to accept the police order of which one is a beneficiary. Therefore, one opts to stand alongside those who have no part in the police order in the formation of a political subject that undercuts the very classifications of that order.

The significance of this approach to solidarity is that it cuts through the stale debates on the left about the relation between those who are oppressed and those who struggle on their behalf. On the one hand, there are, among those who work in solidarity groups, people who "know what is best" for the oppressed groups: how they should struggle, what their goals should be, how they can integrate themselves into mainstream society. On the other hand, there are those among oppressed groups who seek to marginalize those in solidarity with them because "they just don't understand" what it is like to suffer a particular oppression. What these approaches share is an acquiescence to the police order's distinction between *us* and *them*. Among its goals, a democratic politics seeks to eliminate precisely the distinction upon which such disagreements are founded. The issue is not one of how those who are oppressed and those who stand in solidarity with them are to relate to each other. It is how people can form a political subject of democratic action that undercuts the particular oppression itself.

We have seen how democratic politics, how the project of active equality, works in a negative sense, through dissensus and declassification. We have not yet defined the equality out of which people act. Is this equality an empty category? Can we say nothing about it except that it undercuts police orders and their identifications? Recent French philosophy has often worked with terms that operate to resist positive characterization. Think of Derrida's *differance*, Deleuze's difference, Nancy's singular plural, Badiou's multiple. These are terms that resist conceptual articulation. Is equality one of these, or is it something else? I would like to argue that it is, in some sense, both. On the one hand, there is a simple positive characterization of equality that Rancière offers. On the other, this simple positive characterization hides a deeper affinity with the terms mobilized by other French thinkers.

To see the positive characterization, we can start with a story that Rancière tells in his book *The Ignorant Schoolmaster*. With the restoration of the French monarchy after the Revolution, a revolutionary named Joseph Jacotot is forced to flee France and settles in Flanders. Unfortunately, he does not speak a word of Flemish, but nevertheless he takes a position as a school teacher. The only book he has is a dual-language edition of *Telemachus*, in French and Flemish. He must teach from that book, navigating the divide between his French and his students' Flemish. In the course of teaching, he assigns the students a paper on *Telemachus*, to be written in French, a language they do not know and for which their only resource is this book that is common between them. To his surprise, Jacotot finds that the students write papers that are not only adequate but excellent.

From this, Jacotot draws a conclusion. People are equally intelligent. The differences between them lie not in their intelligence but in their attention. Rancière writes, "What stultifies the common people is not the lack of instruction, but the belief in the inferiority of their intelligence."[24] The task of a teacher, then, is not one of teaching students what they don't know. They are as capable of finding out what they don't know as the teacher is. The task is one of motivating them to attend to their work so that their equal intelligence will have an opportunity to find expression.

The presupposition of equality, the presupposition that founds any democratic politics, is the presupposition that people are, in some sense, equally intelligent.

To presuppose that people are equally intelligent is not to presuppose that they are capable of the same SAT scores or that anyone could have formulated the theory of relativity. It is to presuppose that each person, anyone and everyone as Rancière puts it, is capable of speaking to one another, understanding one another, reasoning with one another. It is to presuppose that we are equally capable of putting together meaningful lives in interaction with one another, and to rise to the tasks that that life puts before us. The equality of intelligence, then, is not a numerical equality. We can say that it is qualitative: each of us, unless we have been severely damaged, possesses the quality of being able to consider and act upon our world in such a way as to create a life that has significance for us.

When addressing the equality of intelligence, Rancière often privileges the linguistic character of the intellect. "Spectacular or otherwise, political activity is always a mode of expression that undoes the perceptible divisions of the police order by implementing a basically heterogeneous assumption . . . the equality of any speaking being with any other speaking being."[25] The equality here appears to be that of speech. Anyone who can speak is the equal of anyone else who can speak. The example of Jacotot and his students testifies to this privileging. It is the ability of students to speak, or at least to communicate in language, that impresses upon Jacotot the equality of their intelligence.

This particular privileging of speech is evident in a "proof" of equality Rancière occasionally offers. If someone is given an order by another who considers him or her an inferior, the assumption is that the "inferior" understands the order, and thus can speak, and is thus the equal of the person giving the order.[26] Therefore, the division into superiors and inferiors is a not only contingent; it is, in a sense, self-contradictory. It presupposes the equality it seeks to deny.

In one sense, the privileging of speech is reasonable. If one is to act in the name of equality, it would seem that one must be able adequately to name it. "A word has all the power originally given it. This power is in the first place the power to create a space where equality can state its own claim; it is spoken of and written about. It must therefore be verifiable. Here is the basis for a practice that sets itself the task of verifying this equality."[27] But must the basis for the equality of intelligence lie in speech? Can one act out of the presupposition of equality without calling it such? It seems at least possible to do so. The presupposition of equality does not have to be consciously recognized in order for it to be effective, in order for a democratic politics to occur. It is usually explicit, but it can be implicit.

To see why, let us return to the example of the French tailors' strike. Their actions constituted a challenge to those who would oppress them and yet still retained a commitment to the preamble of the French Charter of 1830. But did they strike specifically in the name of equality? More important, did they need to in order for their actions to be an exercise in democratic politics? Suppose their actions arose out of a more inchoate sense that they were being dispossessed by their bosses. Suppose that they did not say to themselves, "We are their equals," but rather simply acted in such a way that *we*, looking back at them, say of them that they were acting from the presupposition of equality. Would theirs not still have been an expression of equality, even without their having thought of it in that way? One might respond by saying that to feel a sense of dispossession implies that one considers oneself an equal, or more nearly so, to those dispossessing one. Agreed: that is the point. Although the presupposition of equality is often explicit in a democratic politics, it can remain implicit. It can exist even where it is not spoken, even where the term *equality*, or some cognate term, is not consciously invoked by those participating in the expression.

We have seen examples of this in recent politics. During the first Palestinian *intifada*, Palestinians youths threw stones at Israeli tanks and jeeps. Their aim was clear: to end the Israeli occupation of their land. Yet the language of equality, although everywhere implicit, was not appealed to in public discourse. Of course the youths did not think their stones equal to the bullets of the Israeli soldiers. More to the point, they did not actively *think* of themselves, militarily or otherwise, as their equals. (Perhaps some did, but equality was not the term framing the conflict.) They demonstrated their equality passionately, through their willingness to confront their adversary in a situation of extreme military *inequality*. However, equality, although everywhere present, was not the discursive frame within which these demonstrations took place. We might say that the equality was lived rather than spoken.

If this is right, then Rancière need not privilege speech in his evocation of the equality of intelligence. That equality is intimately bound to speech is undeniable. It is hard to imagine a non-speaking being acting out of the presupposition of equality. However, the equality of intelligence is not reducible to speech. Instead, it concerns the ability to consider and carry out life projects, to participate in the construction of a life. What a democratic politics presupposes is not simply "the equality of any speaking being with any other speaking being." It is the equality of every being that can participate in the reflective construction of a life. Rancière writes, just below his passage on the power of words, "How can one verify words? Essentially, through one's actions. These actions must be organized like a proof, a system of reasons."[28] We can ratify this, and indeed see the tailors' strike as a proof, a system reasons, establishing the presupposition of equality. But the words that are verified need not be the tailors' words. They can be the words implied by whatever beliefs the tailors' brought to their action. They can be the entailment of words – or actions – rather than the words themselves.

In traditional philosophical literature, the ability to participate in the reflective construction of a life is often called *autonomy*. Rancière does not appeal to this term, and we will follow him here. The term carries the baggage of liberal individualism which is far from the project of any democratic politics. It is often used to refer to an ability to act under one's own control, regardless of what is happening around one. What a democratic politics recognizes, among other things, is that there is no such thing as an autonomous individual in the sense that traditional theorists like Thomas Hobbes or John Locke would have us believe. We are all born to police orders. And if we resist those orders by engaging in a democratic politics, it is not as a collection of individual subjects, but rather through the formation of a collective subject whose members share nothing other than their own equality.

But here we are faced with a question. Rancière seems to build his case for the equality of intelligence on one man's experience and a quick proof that assuming someone understands an order is tantamount to an admission of equality. These seem thin reeds to hold the weight he seeks to place upon them. Can he offer us anything more in the way of a proof of equal intelligence? Alternatively, ought we to seek such a proof? Is that Rancière's aim? Is Rancière *arguing* here that people are equally intelligent?

He is not. He offers the equality of intelligence not as a conclusion to an argument, but rather as a starting point for politics. Even his informal "proof" of the equality of intelligence, if we accept it, offers no reason to believe that intelligence is equal. It offers only a reason to believe that the person who issues the order is committed to it. What is the motivation for the presupposition of the equality of intelligence then? It is in order to see where this presupposition might lead. "[O]ur problem," he writes, "isn't proving that all intelligence is equal. It's seeing what can be done under that presupposition. And for this, it's enough for us that the opinion be possible – that is, that no opposing truth be proved."[29]

This might seem an odd position to take. He stakes a democratic politics not on any proposition he can convince us is true, or that he even offers any but the flimsiest of evidence for. What motivation should we have to base a politics on this? In order to answer this question, we must first keep in mind how minimal the assumption of the equality of intelligence is. It does not concern comparative intellectual abilities. Rather, it concerns the ability of each of us, in concert with others, to engage in the project of a reflective construction of lives. Bearing this in mind, the assumption of the equality of intelligence is not peculiar to Rancière's approach to politics. It is, in fact, a necessary presupposition of any progressive politics.

A progressive politics must, if it is indeed to be progressive, take issue with the current hierarchies in place in a society. Whether those hierarchies are economic, political, or social, a progressive politics argues that they are unjust and must be changed. If so, such a politics is also committed to the idea that those who are oppressed in these hierarchies ought to be allowed greater participation in governing the economic, political, or social arrangements than they currently possess. But that commitment brings with it another one: that those who are oppressed are *capable* of greater participation, that they will not make things worse for themselves through such participation. And therein lies the presupposition of the equality of intelligence.

A Marxist does not argue that the workers ought to control the means of production without also committing himself or herself to the view that the workers can indeed adequately control those means. The argument is never: the workers are incapable of controlling the means of production – they lack the intelligence of the bourgeoisie – but nevertheless it is unjust for them to be denied control. Similarly, and even more obviously, those who argue for equal rights for African Americans or women or gays presuppose that these groups are capable of exercising those rights as intelligently as those who already possess them.

Now one might take issue with this latter example, since it is not concerned with a democratic politics but rather, in accordance with the last chapter, with distribution. Indeed it is. That is the crux of the claim being pressed here. It is not simply a democratic politics as we have defined it here – a politics of active equality – but instead *any* progressive politics, any politics critical of current arrangements for the sake of an oppressed people – a part that has not part – that is committed to the presupposition of the equality of intelligence. This presupposition is not peculiar to Rancière's politics. What he has done is to isolate a commitment common to all progressive politics, and then follow it further than many (for example, Iris Young) have, to see where it may lead. And where it leads is to the emergence of a democratic politics, a politics of people who act on the presupposition of their equality.

Rancière's commitment to the equality of intelligence is central to the formation of a democratic politics. If dissensus and declassification form the negative core of a politics of active equality, then the equality of intelligence forms its positive core. There are many, however, who will resist this positive core. The presupposition of the equality of intelligence may face a number of objections, particularly in light of recent political theory. It is worth pausing over three objections that might be raised to this positive core of a democratic politics. The first and most obvious one is that people are not equally intelligent, even in Rancière's minimal sense. The second and third stem from developments in recent French political thought. The second objection is that by invoking the presupposition of equality, Rancière returns us to an essentialism that is rejected by many of his contemporaries in recent Continental thought. In addressing this objection, I will redeem a promissory note issue above, where I said that while in one sense the positive articulation of the concept of equality is unlike a-conceptual developments in recent French thought (Derrida, Deleuze, Nancy, Badiou), in another sense it does have deep affinities with them. The third objection, related to the second, is that by ascribing a politics of equality retrospectively to earlier political movements, especially those that do not arise consciously in the name of equality, Rancière's approach to a democratic politics is a-historical. It is insensitive to historical differences among political movements. This objection is like the second one in that it seems to imply that Rancière's thought is wedded to an essentialism. However, as we will see, it unfolds differently and requires a different response.

In responding to the first objection, we need to be clear about what that objection itself must be committed to. If the equality of intelligence means that people can reflectively conduct their lives with others, then the objection must deny this minimal commitment. This is, at best, counterintuitive. There certainly are people who, for one reason or another, are incapable of this. People with severe Down's syndrome or mental retardation cannot, without much assistance, conduct their lives with others, and they cannot do so very reflectively. However, those people are also unlikely to be the subjects of political action. The question, then, is whether those who have not suffered significant damage are to be considered of equal intelligence in Rancière's sense. To put the point in terms Aristotle was fond of, the issue is whether people "in general and for the most part" can be said to be equally intelligent.

Here the counterintuitive character of the objection comes to the fore. Rancière does not seek to prove that people are equally intelligent. He seeks only to establish it as a possibility for politics. The objection that people cannot in general and for the most part reflectively consider and create lives alongside others has gone no way toward removing that possibility. Quite the opposite. Since the objection is counterintuitive, it would need some support if it is to be ranged against Rancière's position. Moreover, as Rancière points out, the presupposition of the equality of intelligence can be maintained as long as the opposite has not been proven. The bare challenge offered by this objection cannot stand by itself.

What would constitute evidence against Rancière's position? It cannot come from standardized intelligence tests, and it cannot come from some form of a priori argument. Does this mean that the presupposition is immune to evidence? Not at all. The evidence to tell against it would have to come from the consequences of a democratic politics. When people engage in a democratic politics, when they act out of the presupposition of equality, do their actions rise to the presupposed level of equality? When workers take over factories or indigenous Latin American groups form self-sustaining communities or African Americans occupy positions previously reserved for whites, do they do worse than if they were in more hierarchical (or further down in traditional hierarchical) arrangements? And in addressing this question, we must ask it not from the position of capitalist calculation but from the position of how a meaningful life goes. The question is not, do these movements make people more productive? It is rather, do these movements make the lives of the people participating in them better or worse?

These are difficult questions, but they are not immune to evidence. We can approach them sociologically and historically. The misfortune here is not that Rancière's view cannot be tested, but that there is so little ground upon which to test them. Democratic politics, as Rancière tells us, happens rarely. And when it does, it is usually either defeated or absorbed into the police order. In the latter case, things often improve for those engaged in the politics. Reforms are made. But the democratic character of the politics more often then not quickly fades, and there is little ground left upon which to ask the question of whether the equality that informed the struggle is a justifiable presupposition.

We cannot perform the tests of such a challenge here. It would bring us too far afield. However, I am skeptical the challenge would receive much empirical support. If we consider examples of democratic politics, from the Indian struggle against the British to the civil rights movement in the U.S. to the first Palestinian *intifada* to the many workers' movements for collective ownership, we see that the lives of participants were not diminished by their struggle. If anything, they were enhanced. It is struggles characterized by hierarchy rather than democratic struggles that most often lead to an impoverishment in the lives of their participants.

The second objection is that the presupposition of the equality of intelligence is essentialist in a sense that has been rejected by many of

Rancière's contemporaries. One option open to those who want to reply to this objection is that his contemporaries are mistaken and that essentialism is an important element of a democratic politics. I will not take this path, in part because I believe that the anti-essentialists are on to something important.[30] Essentialism has a way of excluding people, of setting up a standard for who one should be or what one should do, usually a standard derived from a well-positioned group or class, and then marginalizing those who cannot or will not embrace the standard. Many essentialisms take the usual behavior or social practices or cognitive orientations of a dominant group and assume that those must be the universal standards against which other behavior or practices or cognition must be measured – and found wanting. Feminist thought has called attention to this dynamic in the history of philosophy and elsewhere. The marginalization that arises from it has been a motivation for many recent French theorists. What we must ask of Rancière, then, is whether his embrace of the equality of intelligence forms an essentialism of the kind that justifiably worries many of his contemporaries.

We should recall here that a democratic politics is neither a matter of coming to consensus nor a matter of distribution. If people are equally intelligent and are to act out of the presupposition of that equal intelligence, it is neither to confirm any particular identity nor to propose one. Nor is it to say that people are all the same in the sense that would justify a particular distributive pattern. It is instead to refuse the identities that are on offer, the roles that have been proffered by the current police arrangement. "The difference that political disorder inscribes in the police order can thus, at first glance, be expressed as the difference between subjectification and identification."[31] To put the point another way, it is not in the name of an identity or of a sameness that equality is acted out; it is, in the term that is often used by Rancière's contemporaries, in the name of difference. Equality, Rancière insists, does not unify; it declassifies. A democratic politics is not based simply on an assumption with a different conceptual content from the current police order – that of the equality of intelligence – but, following from that, on a heterogeneity to the established police order that is not recuperable in the form of a different police order. To put the point another way, the assumption of equal intelligence does not tag anyone with an essential identity; rather it gives them the ability to refuse the identities imposed upon them by the hierarchical order in which they have been raised. To refuse these identities is not a form of essentialism, but rather its opposite.

In this, although not in many other ways, Rancière's concept of equal intelligence is like Jean-Paul Sartre's concept of freedom. Sartre rejects all essentialisms in the name of human freedom. If we are radically free, then we have no essence. One might want to accuse Sartre here of simply substituting one essence for others. If our essence isn't that of, for example, being made in God's image, it is instead that of possessing radical freedom. Such an accusation would miss Sartre's point. The rejection of essentialism is not a rejection of the term *essence*. It is a rejection of what the history of essentialism requires: the belief that humans must or ought to be one way rather than any another. Rancière's appeal to the equality of intelligence implies the same rejection, even if the framework of his thought is historical and political rather than, as with Sartre, ontological.

There is both an affinity with and a divergence between the presupposition of equality and the traditional liberal concept of autonomy. The affinity lies in the idea that for both, one does not have to be any particular way. The way one has been made to be by the social order is contingent. "The foundation of politics is not in fact more a matter of convention than of nature: it is the absence of foundation, the sheer contingency of any social order. There is politics simply because no social order is based on nature, no divine law regulates human society."[32] This is the rejection of essentialism. In that sense, Rancière's democratic politics shares with liberalism the anti-essentialism it also shares with much of recent French thought. The divergence with the concept of autonomy lies in the fact that for the latter, the alternative to essentialism is self-creation. Therein lies the individualism of liberal theory. For a democratic politics, the alternative to essentialism – an alternative opened up by the sheer contingency of any social order – is a collective assertion or expression based upon the presupposition of equality.

The third objection is that utilizing the concept of equality to describe all democratic politics is ahistorical. Rancière says that all politics worthy of the name has been a matter of equality. His historical examples range from ancient slave revolts[33] to nineteenth-century workers' movements to contemporary politics. Doesn't this sweeping application of the concept of equality betray an inability to distinguish radically different historical periods and struggles? Do we really want to say that the political struggle of the *sans-papiers* in Europe is fundamentally the same as that of the slaves of classical Greece? This would seem to be an anachronistic reading of history, applying a term that is of relatively local and recent vintage to political movements that are divergent in time and character.

This objection might be seen as associated with the orientation of thinkers like Foucault and Thomas Kuhn. For both Foucault and Kuhn, history is more a matter of breaks than continuities. What comes after is not solely a development of what came before. We cannot simply look from our perspective and say that what was going on earlier is simply a more primitive version of what is happening now. That would be an uncritical projection of our self-understanding into the past.

Let me cite two brief examples here. Foucault argues in *Discipline and Punish*[34] that the history of punishment changes radically from its earlier incarnation in torture to its later one in rehabilitation. This is not simply a progress in our recognition of how to deter crime or make punishment more humane. It is also tied up with the emergence of a project of normalization. Rehabilitation is a different project from torture. It is not just a demonstration of the sovereign's power, but instead is dedicated to creating normal, docile subjects of an entire population. Where torture was barbaric and yet infrequent, normalization, in its alliance with rehabilitation, is more subtle and pervasive. To read torture as simply a cruder form of punishment than rehabilitation is to miss the historical and political character of both.

Kuhn's concern is more epistemological than political. He finds the history of science burdened with a false sense of continuity and progress. He argues, for example in his famous essay *The Structure of Scientific Revolutions*, that the concept of mass is not just refined when we change from a Newtonian to an Einsteinian physics. "[T]he physical referents of these Einsteinian concepts are by no means identical with those of the Newtonian concepts that bear the same name. (Newtonian mass is conserved; Einsteinian mass is convertible with energy. Only at low relative velocities may the two be measured in the same way, and even then they must not be conceived to be the same.)"[35] While Kuhn's later writings abandon the idea that earlier concepts are entirely incommensurable with the proceeding ones, he retains a commitment to the historical specificity of concepts and the scientific orientation and practices in which they are embedded.

One response to this objection would be to deny that the concept of equality is historically specific in the way the objection supposes. Equality plays an important role at least as far back as Aristotle's *Politics*. In fact, it is central to his idea of justice. "Thus it is thought that justice is equality; and so it is, but not for all persons, only for those that are equal. Inequality also is thought to be just; and so it is, but not for all, only for the unequal."[36] This response offers something, but it is not enough. Kuhn, for instance, argues that the same term, ex. *mass*, can be used in different ways at different times and with different meanings. This will be even more so between terms translated from ancient Greek (*isos* in this case, which is often translated as *equal* or *fair*) and current usage. Therefore, the mere fact that there has been some continuity of an idea like equality does not by itself show that Rancière has avoided anachronism.

Nevertheless, it would be a misunderstanding of Rancière's position to say that he has run foul of the strictures imposed by the writings of thinkers like Foucault and Kuhn. To see why, we must recognize first that their thought involves elements of *both* continuity and discontinuity. This does not mean that we must embrace the idea of progress that they criticize. Continuity is a descriptive term, while progress is a normative one. Foucault and Kuhn offer compelling arguments against a naïve historical progressivism, but they do so in part on the basis of retaining certain concepts as historically continuous. In fact, their historical approaches would be inconceivable without an appeal to certain concepts which they take as, if I may be permitted the term, *transhistorical*. Their histories rely on certain transhistorical concepts in order to show the historical specificity of other concepts and practices.

In *Discipline and Punish*, for example, both torture and rehabilitation are punitive practices. Punishment is the transhistorical concept operative in that history.[37] Rehabilitation may diverge from torture in several important ways, but nevertheless it retains a continuity with torture, since it emerges from the same broad project – that of punishment – that torture engaged in. In fact, without this continuity, it would not make sense to say that rehabilitation diverged from torture. Unless they were part of the same history of punishment, then rehabilitation would no more have diverged from torture than it would have diverged from bloodletting or the Feasts of Fools. It would simply have been something else, another practice in another arena. In order for anything like a *history* to be written, there must be both continuity and discontinuity. Without continuity there is no story, of either divergence or convergence. Without discontinuity there is no temporal change. Foucault and Kuhn often focus on the discontinuities, but have continuities implicit in their work. Foucault himself recognizes this, even in his early work, where he emphasizes discontinuity. "These pre-existing forms of continuity," he writes, "all these syntheses that are accepted without question, must remain in suspense. They must not be definitively rejected, of course, but the tranquility with which they are accepted must be disturbed."[38] What motivates Foucault's and Kuhn's work is not so much the rejection of any concepts of continuity – and transhistorical concepts – as a rejection of an uncritical progressivist approach to history.[39]

The concept of equality serves as a transhistorical concept in Rancière's work. In looking historically at various political struggles, some stand out as grouping themselves into a certain category. They involve more than just pleading by the oppressed, and are structured by something more than a desire for reform. Those struggles seem to have, implicitly or explicitly, an embrace of equality at their core. They may or may not seek equal treatment by those in power, but in either case they are best understood as emerging out of a presupposition of equality. "Equality is not a given that politics then presses into service, an essence embodied in the law or a goal politics sets itself the task of attaining. It is only an assumption that needs to be discerned within the practices implementing it."[40] This discernment does not, of course, have to have a binary character: either these struggles do or do not presuppose equality. It can be a matter of the more and the less. However, those struggles that seem more deeply or more explicitly to have presupposed equality – to have utilized the presupposition of the equality of intelligence in a declassifying way and in dissensus from a particular police order – stand out across history as models of a democratic politics.

Rancière's concept of equality, then, does not render his work ahistorical. Were he to try to offer a fine-grained analysis of political movements that sees them each as instantiating a particular and well-specified model of struggle, then he might be accused of being ahistorical. However, that is not what he does. To the contrary, Rancière is sensitive to historical differences among various political struggles and movements. His concept of equality functions like Foucault's concept of punishment, as a marker of sameness in a history of differences. If Foucault's concept of punishment ties together two divergent practices into a single historical thread, Rancière's concept of equality ties together divergent struggles into a single thematic thread. Nevertheless, since historical perspective requires both continuities and discontinuities, Rancière's application of the term equality does not violate the strictures imposed by the perspectives Foucault and Kuhn have opened.

One might object that there is an important difference between the historical continuities in Foucault and Kuhn on the one hand and Rancière's concept of equality on the other. For the former, there is a chronological bond between what comes before and what comes after. Rehabilitation and normalization change a previously existing practice; the interpretation of mass retains a concept from the previous configuration. With equality, there is no historical continuity. It appears at diverse times and in diverse geographical locations. Therefore, there is nothing to latch onto to create the kinds of continuities found in Foucault's and Kuhn's work.

This objection misses what is at work in Foucault's and Kuhn's interpretations, indeed in any historical interpretation. One must always find the similarities and differences from the standpoint of one's own concepts and categories. It is impossible to step completely outside one's own way of understanding the past. One can break with the past (otherwise there could never be a politics of dissensus), but to step outside it entirely is impossible. Foucault utilizes the concept of punishment, and Kuhn the concept of mass, because these are concepts of which we have a particular understanding. They show how such concepts did not always operate in the way they operate for us now. But to do so they must, as we have seen, appeal to both continuity and discontinuity. It is the same with equality. Rancière finds similarities among the divergent practices and understandings of our political past. He "discerns within the practices implementing it" a presupposition of equality. Doing so does not require historical continuity. It does not require that there be a single thread of equality that has woven its way through our history. It only requires that the understanding of equality we have now can be seen in its similarities and differences in past practices. This is no different in kind from what Foucault and Kuhn do. Indeed, it is a requirement placed upon any project whose goal is to arrive at an understanding of the past.

Rancière has offered us a presupposition that characterizes a democratic politics. But his aim is more than political analysis. He is interested not simply in history, but in struggle. Who is his audience, then? Who is it that should embrace the presupposition of equality? Those who are seeing what can be done. Those who will act under this presupposition: the people who struggle, the part that has no part. And there are, as we have seen, many parts that have no part.

But to whom is the demonstration of equality made? If the part that has no part is demonstrating equality and displaying the contingency of a particular police order, who is the object of this demonstration? It is perhaps above all to themselves. To take oneself as an equal being and to act on the presupposition of equality is to demonstrate that equality to oneself. "This is the demonstration of a struggle for equality which can never be merely a demand upon the other, nor a pressure put upon him, but always simultaneously a proof given to oneself. This is what 'emancipation' means."[41]

Students of the history of political struggle will immediately recognize the significance of Rancière's thought here. From Steven Biko's Black Consciousness movement in South Africa to the first *intifada* in Palestine to the development of Queer Studies, the self-demonstration of the equality of the demos is an inescapable moment of any politics of resistance. The equality of the demos must be shown, first and foremost, to itself.

There is a danger here as well, one that Rancière's thought takes pains to avoid. The danger lies in the movement from the demonstration of equality to identity politics. There are many ways for the demos to demonstrate equality. What they all converge on, however, is the possession or expression of something that acts as a motivation for thinking oneself equal. (I use the term *motivation* instead of *justification* in order to keep alive the recognition that equality is, ultimately, not to be proven but to be presupposed.) The development of jazz, for instance, can motivate a sense of musical equality in African Americans.

The danger of these motivations is that they coalesce into some view of the essential character of the demos. Then you have identity politics. Identity politics does not undercut the operation of police order; it simply substitutes another police order for the one that is being rejected. Or, to put the matter another way, identity politics does not declassify; it reclassifies. To demonstrate equality is not to impose a new order, as though the old order had simply been mistaken in its categorization. It is, as Rancière says, to show the contingency of any order.

The demonstration of equality, the collective action out of a presupposition of equality, is a process of what Rancière calls *subjectification*. In demonstrating equality, one becomes a subject. For those familiar with Foucault's thought, the term *subjectification* will have a negative connotation. Subjectification, for Foucault, concerns the processes by which institutions and practices turn one into a docile subject. Rancière uses the term in a different way, much closer to that of the thought of Alain Badiou. To become a subject is to make oneself appear, to create oneself as a subject, to impress oneself on the scene. "By *subjectification* I mean the production through a series of actions of an instance and a capacity for enunciation not previously identifiable within a given field of experience, whose identification is of a pair with the reconfiguration of experience."[42]

To become a subject is one side of the coin, the other side of which is the creation of a dissensus. When one becomes a subject, one does so by means of rejecting the classification of the police order; and one does that by acting and speaking in a way that demonstrates an equality that runs counter to the inequality of the classification. To become a subject is to make oneself appear where there had previously been only categories, and indeed categories that rendered one or one's experience more or less invisible. The declassification of democratic politics is an aesthetic phenomenon; it makes something appear that had been there before. To engage in a democratic politics is not to discover a subject of politics; it is to create one. Equality is not received. It is made. In fact, Rancière might argue, equality cannot be received, because to receive equality is already to be less than equal to the one who bestows it.

A democratic politics is a politics of the formation of subjects. This is what Rancière means when he writes that, "Politics does not happen because the poor oppose the rich. It is the other way around: politics (that is, the interruption of the simple effects of domination by the rich) causes the poor to exist as an entity."[43] There are no pre-given interests or pre-given classes or pre-given struggles. To think that there are is to return to the idea of classification that Rancière's thought cuts against. Interests and classes and struggles arise because a group of people decides to make itself a subject, because a group of people decides to demonstrate its equality. To say that politics causes the poor to exist is not to claim that politics impoverishes people. It is to claim that the poor as a group with its own struggle and interests begins to appear with politics. Without politics, Rancière writes, "There is only the order of domination or the disorder of revolt."[44]

If this is so, then the subjectification of politics is necessarily an interpersonal one. (It is also ethical, a point to which we will return in Chapter 4.) One does not emancipate oneself politically by oneself. Politics is not a matter of the assertion of personal autonomy. That would be the disorder of revolt. Politics, which we have begun to call democratic politics and Rancière himself often calls the practice of democracy, is a matter of community. "Democracy is the community of sharing, in both senses of the term: membership in a single world which can only be expressed in adversarial terms, and a coming together which can only occur in conflict."[45] Or, as he puts it elsewhere, "A community of equals is an insubstantial community of individuals engaged in the ongoing creation of equality. Anything else paraded under this banner is either a trick, a school or a military unit."[46]

Subjectification, in its self-creation, has a complex relation to time. A people in struggle become a subject, they act out of a collective sense of their equality. However, although that sense of one's equality is bound to the structure of the struggle itself, it is projected backwards in time. "Thus, equality is not simply that presupposition which ascribes social congregation in the last instance to the community of speaking beings, as to a principle necessarily forgotten; for it is manifest in the recurring rupture which, by projecting the egalitarian presupposition back to a point anterior to itself, endows it with a social significance."[47] To engage in a democratic politics, in the politics of equality, is not simply to say, or to act as though one were saying, "We are now equal." It is to structure the past in light of equality. To act democratically is to always have been equal. The democratic political subject creates itself in the moment of its struggle, but the presupposition of its struggle is ascribed to a past that justifies it retrospectively.

The practice of a democratic politics, the creation of a political subject, while it is above all a demonstration to oneself and the formation of a community, is not simply an affair of self-involvement. Rancière's use of a term like *dissensus* indicate this. The practice of equality occurs in a situation of the inegalitarian classification of the police order. Thus a politics can be more or less effective in creating change. As we have seen, the "verification [of equality] becomes 'social', causes equality to have a real social effect, only when it mobilizes an *obligation* to hear." We ought not, however, to confuse having social effects with the existence of politics. A politics may or may not effect change. It is not in the consequences but in the acting out of a presupposition of equality that politics occurs. Politics begins and ends in a dissensus, a dissensus that disrupts the police order. Whether those who benefit from that order will ultimately be made to hear, whether they can be mobilized toward an obligation to hear, is an important question, even a crucial one. But it is not a question of whether a democratic politics exists. A democratic politics is defined by the actions and the understandings of those who struggle, not by the effects upon or actions taken by those the police order supports. Otherwise put, politics lies in the creation of the poor, not in the magnanimity of the rich.

Let us return, then, to the situation with which we started. What are we to make of what happened in the wake of Kashef White's death?

We can first look at the reaction of the city, for it falls neatly within the police order Rancière describes. One evening soon after the meeting following Kashef's death, I attended a City Council meeting. During the open session, where anyone is allowed to address the Council, I cited some events and statistics that indicated that perhaps there might be a problem of racism in the city. I was interrupted by a Council member who told me pointedly that I was trying to stir up trouble when the city needed healing. Those of us with memories long enough to remember accusations of "outside agitators" during the civil rights movement will hear a resonance here, and they would not be mistaken. However, beneath this association lies the city's attempt to unify, to deny dissensus, and to return to the categories it had previously embraced. Throughout the period of organizing, the city was steadfast in its denial that there was a problem of racism in Clemson, as though there were any city in America where that were not a problem, and as though a rural town in South Carolina could not possibly have racial issues.

How to prevent dissensus, since this was the threat the city faced? Given the events, denial would not, by itself, be enough. So the city turned toward what is commonly called co-optation. This is where the paving of roads, the youth scholarships, the task force, come in. Again, we might read these superficially, and not incorrectly, as cynical attempts to placate Clemson's African American population. But let us ask, what would the placating itself achieve? It retains a particular unity in which everyone has his or her place. And it does so in a particular manner. By the very act of distributing goods, the city maintains inequality. There are those capable of distributing, those who have the means to give to those who do not. And there are those, the less equal, who receive these distributions but have no part in the community's deliberations. Distribution itself is of the police order of inequality. It should not be surprising, then, that while the city offered many things, it never gave exactly what was demanded. To give what was demanded would be to admit equality, to recognize the legitimacy of the demands that were made. To refuse what was demanded while giving what was not demanded allowed the city to retain its relationship of inequality with the African American community.

Rancière writes, in an analysis we can only gesture at here, that speech can be recognized *as* speech, which recognizes the equality of the speaker, or as merely sounds, cries, grunts without meaning.[48] The latter refuses to recognize the equality of speaking subjects. It denies speech to the speaker, and allows one to speak in the speaker's stead. The city sought, doggedly and persistently, to deny speech to the African American community, and to refuse to recognize it when it was offered. One hot summer evening the City Council, after months of cajoling, agreed to hold a meeting in a local community center with the African American community. When faced with complaints not only about the police but also about inadequate housing, parks, lighting, etc., the mayor repeatedly interrupted the speakers to announce that the meeting was to concern only the police – this, as though the connections between the police and other forms of neglect, obvious to everyone else in the room, were irrelevant intrusions. Finally, one community resident asked, "Why are we talking to you since you can't even hear what we're saying?" Indeed, Rancière would doubtlessly have said.

What about the African American community, though? Since the force of Rancière's approach lay in its treatment of those who struggle, can we learn anything from him here?

After a couple of years of struggle, with slowly diminishing involvement, we decided to run someone from the African American community for City Council. Not only did we lose, but the voter turnout in the African American precincts was no better than it usually was. Although we knocked on almost every door and were warmly received by many, that reception did not turn into votes. It was soon after that that many of us drifted away from the struggle. I, for one, had the feeling of failure.

It was several years later, when I began to read Rancière's work, that I came to understand where the failure lay. In our organizing we received much passive support. One could feel that Clemson's African Americans were rooting for us. But that did not turn into participation. I was always puzzled by this, since, as I explained over and over again in organizational meetings, in a small college town where the university would be insistent on maintaining the veneer of racial harmony, an organized African American community would be in a very powerful position to effect change. People understood this argument, I am sure. But, after the initial flush of anger at the events surrounding Kashef's death, they did not join in.

At the time, I chalked it all up to a lack of hope, physical isolation, and to a history of intimidation. But there was something else going on, something that brought together these various elements. The African American community of Clemson was unable to operate on the presupposition of equality. It was unable, perhaps because of its history, to see itself as equal to the white community. When asked about my experience, I often said that Clemson's African Americans struck me as living as though the civil rights movement had never passed through the town. What were the implications of that? The civil rights movement was a dissensus that operated out of a presupposition of equality. It is perhaps one of the finest examples in our history of such a dissensus. To sit at a lunch counter and order lunch alongside whites is as profound demonstration of equality as one could ask. It is this that never took place in Clemson's African American community.

We won a number of concessions, to be sure. They were not the ones we demanded, but they were substantial in their way. In the end, however, politics did not happen in Clemson. It may have showed itself, in the few weeks after Kashef's death, in prospect. But that prospect never took hold. What we achieved in the end was a better police order.

Rancière's writings warn us of this. Politics happens very little or rarely. What happened in Clemson is not so foreign to what happens in many places, and it can stand as a lesson in the rarity of politics. On the other hand, by understanding the failure of politics in instances such as this, we can also understand the hope of politics, and not mistake it or ignore it when it does happen. We are all familiar with the many travesties that have paraded themselves under the banner of a liberatory politics. To keep sight of politics, however, is to keep sight of what Rancière calls subjectification. It is to keep sight of a people living democracy, not as an end to which they are entitled, but as a presupposition out of which they act. It is to keep sight of the dissensus that will rend the fabric of a given police order. Finally, it is to watch, and perhaps if one is lucky to participate in, an equality that needs no other moment as its horizon because the struggle for it and its appearance are one and the same.

Notes

1. Jacques Rancière, *Disagreement.* tr. Julie Rose. Minneapolis: University of Minnesota Press, 1999 (or. pub. 1995), p. 17.
2. Rancière, *Disagreement*, p. 17.
3. Rancière, *Disagreement*, p. 28 (translation modified).
4. Michel Foucault, *Sécurité, territoire, population: Cours au Collège de France (1977–1978).* Paris: Gallimard, 2004, p. 347.
5. Michel Foucault, "Omnes et Singulatum," http://www.tannerlectures. utah.edu/lectures/foucault81.pdf, pp. 251–2
6. Plato, *Republic*, tr. G. M. A. Grube, rev. C. D. C. Reeve. Indianapolis: Hackett, 1992, p. 109 (434a–b).
7. Plato, *Republic*, p. 91 (415a).

8. Rancière, *Disagreement*, p. 65 (translation modified).
9. Rancière, *Disagreement*, p. 70. The quote from Aristotle is from *Politics*, Book 4 1261 a 41-42.
10. Rancière, *Disagreement*, p. 74.
11. Rancière, *Disagreement*, p. 82.
12. Rancière, *Disagreement*, p. 86.
13. In his article "A Leftist Plea for Eurocentrism," Slajov Žižek argues that there are two more forms of the denial of politics: ultra-politics (Carl Schmitt's reduction of politics to warfare) and post-politics (European technocracy). *Critical Inquiry*, Vol. 24, No. 4, Summer, 1998, pp. 988–1009. See also his Afterword to the English translation of Rancière's *The Politics of Aesthetics*, pp. 69–79. On my reading of Rancière, postpolitics would be a form of metapolitics.
14. Rancière, *Disagreement*, p. xii (translation modified).
15. Jacques Rancière, "Ten Theses on Politics," *Theory and Event*, Vol. 5, No. 3, 2001, p. 12.
16. Rancière, "Ten Theses on Politics," p. 10.
17. Rancière, "Ten Theses on Politics," p. 12.
18. Jacques Rancière *On the Shores of Politics*, tr. Liz Heron. London: Verso, 1995 (or. pub. 1992), pp. 32–3.
19. Taylor Branch, *Parting the Waters: America in the King Years 1954–63*. New York: Simon & Schuster, 1988, pp. 271–2.
20. Rancière, *On the Shores of Politics*, p. 86.
21. Rancière, *On the Shores of Politics*, p. 46. In this passage, Rancière cites several ways tensions that go together to form this syllogism. Not only is there a contradiction regarding the prosecution of the tailors' federation, there are two others: between the general treatment of the workers and the Charter and between the prosecutor's attitude toward the workers and the Charter.
22. Rancière, *On the Shores of Politics*, p. 47.
23. Rancière, *Disagreement*, p. 59.
24. Jacques Rancière, *The Ignorant Schoolmaster: Five Lessons in Intellectual Emancipation*, tr. Krisin Ross. Stanford, CA: Stanford University Press, 1991 (or. pub. 1987), p. 39.
25. Rancière, *Disagreement*, p. 30.
26. Cf., ex., *Disagreement*, p. 16.
27. Rancière, *On the Shores of Politics*, p. 47.
28. Rancière, *On the Shores of Politics*, p. 47.
29. Rancière, *The Ignorant Schoolmaster*, p. 46.
30. I discuss this idea at length in *Reconsidering Difference: Nancy, Derrida, Levinas, and Deleuze*. University Park, PA: Penn State Press, 1997.
31. Rancière, *Disagreement*, p. 37.
32. Rancière, *Disagreement*, p. 16 (translation modified).
33. Cf. Rancière, *Disagreement*, p. 12 on the revolt of the Scythian slaves.

34. Michel Foucault, *Discipline and Punish: The Birth of the Prison*. New York: Random House, 1977 (or. pub. 1975).
35. Thomas Kuhn, *The Structure of Scientific Revolutions*. Chicago: University of Chicago Press, 1962, p. 102.
36. Aristotle, *The Politics*, tr. T. A. Sinclair, rev. Trevor J. Saunders. London: Penguin Books, 1981, p. 195 (1280a7).
37. One might argue that *Discipline and Punish* also operates with a transhistorical concept of the body. It is the body that is the site of the different applications of punishment Foucault describes.
38. Michel Foucault, *The Archaeology of Knowledge*. tr. A. M. Sheridan Smith. New York: Harper & Row, 1972 (or. pub. 1969), p. 25.
39. It should be noted that a particular term, for example *punishment*, may be used transhistorically in one history and historically in another. Transhistorical concepts are not a particular set of concepts; they are concepts used in a particular way for particular purposes. It is possible that another historical work would historicize the concept of punishment while holding other concepts as transhistorical.
40. Rancière, *Disagreement*, p. 33 (translation modified).
41. Rancière, *On the Shores of Politics*, p. 48.
42. Rancière, *Disagreement*, p. 35 (translation modified).
43. Rancière, *Disagreement*, p. 11 (translation modified).
44. Rancière, *Disagreement*, p. 12.
45. Rancière, *On the Shores of Politics*, p. 49. On this issue, see also Rancière's discussion of subjectification in his essay "Politics, Identification, and Subjectivization," in *The Identity in Question*, ed. John Rajchman (New York: Routledge, 1995) where he writes that subjectification (translated in that essay as subjectivization) "is the formation of a one that is not a self but is the relation of a self to an other." p. 66.
46. Rancière, *On the Shores of Politics*, p. 84.
47. Rancière, *On the Shores of Politics*, p. 85.
48. Cf. Rancière, *Disagreement*, pp. 21–3.

The Historical Roots of Democratic Politics: Anarchism

The democratic politics proposed by Rancière contrasts sharply with mainstream political thought. It turns its sights away from the part that has a part – the part with access to something to distribute – and toward that part that has no part. Instead of asking what is owed to the demos, it asks what the demos is capable of. The addressee of democratic politics is the people (in its various guises) in its capacity as actor. This chapter asks two historical questions: How should we situate democratic politics? Into what theoretical tradition does it fall?

We must first recognize that Rancière's thought cannot be assimilated to the Marxist tradition. This reflects his personal trajectory. Early in his career, Rancière was a student of the French Marxist Louis Althusser. In fact, he contributed an essay to the seminal Althusserian text *Lire le Capital*, published in 1965.[1]

He breaks from Althusser, however, in the wake of the events of May '68[2] over the latter's opposition to the students and support for a distinction between those who think and those who work or act. For Althusser, there is an autonomy to theoretical practice, an autonomy that justifies the role of the intellectual and that places the worker in a passive position vis-à-vis the intellectual. This, in essence, denies equality to the worker. In his first book, *La Leçon d'Althusser*, published in 1974, Rancière writes, "Althusser needs the opposition between the 'simplicity' of nature and the 'complexity' of history: if production is the affair of the workers, history is too complex for them and must be left to the specialists: the Party and Theory."[3] Although, as Rancière observes, Althusser's views change over the course of his career, and he eventually engages in "self-criticism," he retains a central role for philosophy as distinct from (or within) the class struggle.

When Rancière writes *La Leçon d'Althusser*, he still identifies himself with the Marxist tradition. He feels that Althusser has betrayed the radical equality that Marx himself posits. It is a view that

Rancière begins to question, and his writings progressively distance themselves from Marx. For instance, in *The Philosopher and His Poor*, Rancière displays a more ambivalent relation to Marx than in the earlier book, finding him to turn more toward the scientific views ascribed to his later work by Althusser.

> This science is not the mastery of any object or the formation of any subject. By proclaiming the primacy of production, it paradoxically shuts itself up in the solitude of an art henceforth situated at an infinite distance from all technique. The materialist "reversal," the return from heaven to earth, has the unexpected result of destroying the space of *practice*.[4]

In between the two books, Rancière spends much of his time studying the history of nineteenth-century labor, and begins to formulate the view of active equality discussed in Chapter 2. He discovers in his study not only the political but also the intellectual desires of many in the working class, desires that did not find their way into the Marxist legacy.[5]

One might argue that Althusser's is only one kind of Marxism, a Marxism that finds its roots in the avant-garde approach of Lenin, where there is a strict distinction between the party and the masses. But Marx's legacy need not follow this path. The communist revolution can be conceived as an egalitarian struggle of workers to appropriate the means of production, a struggle that does not require direction by an intellectual class. There is no contradiction between Marxism and active equality. It was once possible, and with the demise of twentieth-century Marxism is again possible, to consider Marxism as a framework for active equality, and to consider the communist revolution as an expression of active equality by the workers.

There is, however, an important theoretical bar to thinking of Marxism this way; a bar that perhaps can be cleared, but a bar nonetheless. The orientation of Marxist thought opens the door to Lenin's avant-garde approach to political change, and to the presupposition of inequality that Leninism brings in its wake. This avantgardism can already be seen in Marx's disagreement with the Russian anarchist Mikhail Bakunin during the First International Workingmen's Association, when Bakunin proposed a more spontaneous revolution from below while Marx favored forming a revolutionary party, of the type later advocated by Lenin.[6] After the demise of the First International, Engels would mock Bakunin and the anarchists' resistance to centralizing power, writing, "Have these gentlemen ever seen a revolution? A revolution is certainly the most authoritarian thing there is; it is the act whereby one part of the population imposes its will on the other by means of rifles, bayonets, and cannon."[7]

Centralization and authoritarianism are no accident. They emerge from the theoretical ground of Marxism. The founding concept for Marx, particularly the later Marx of *Capital*, is exploitation. Exploitation is the extraction of surplus value from the workers. Part of the value of the workers' labor is expropriated by the capitalist, and that expropriated value forms the basis of capitalist profit. The defining conflict around which class struggle is waged is that of exploitation. The worker seeks to reappropriate the labor value that has been exploited. This reappropriation cannot occur within the structure of capitalist economics, since it would leave no place for the capitalist herself. Therefore, only a revolution in economic relations can restore labor value to its rightful owners. When the workers as a whole also become the owners, then there will be a single class of worker/owners, and the history of class conflict will have come to an end.

The concept of exploitation anchors Marx's economic analysis. Other forms of oppression, of what – to anticipate – we will call *domination*, are generally reducible to the conflict of class relations. In a strictly Marxist view, there is no room to allow, for instance, gender oppression or racial discrimination a separate analysis. These problems do not have their own integrity. They are offshoots of the more fundamental problem of capitalist exploitation. This is the force of Marx's view that the fundamental analysis of a society is the analysis of its economic relations. As Marx tells us at the outset of *The Communist Manifesto*, "The history of all hitherto existing society is the history of class struggles."[8] If this is so, then only a revolution that ends class struggles – an economic revolution – will directly address the problem of political oppression.

If there is a single site of oppression, an Archimedean point about which history and struggle turn, then those who are more conversant with that point are the ones best positioned to oversee struggle and resistance. If the fundamental site of oppression lies in the economy, it perhaps falls to those who are adept at economic analysis to take up the task of directing the revolution. It is they who understand how the economy works, therefore how history unfolds, therefore how struggle ought to occur. There is an alliance between a politics that privileges a certain type of oppression and the creation of an avant-garde party. This alliance is not theoretically required; one can maintain both that all oppression is ultimately a matter of exploitation and at the same time that understanding and struggling against exploitation is equally everyone's business. However, the opening for avant-gardism created by a reductionist view of oppression is a large one.

If, by contrast, domination is multifarious, then the distinction between an intellectual class and the masses is more difficult to sustain. When those who have no part are not a single group of people subject to a single type of oppression, then the call for an avantgarde party of those who can oversee oppression and struggle has less grip. The reason for this is not far to seek. It is possible to become an expert in economics, or in racism, or in feminism and sexism, or in immigration policy, or in the history of and attitudes toward homosexuality. But it is unlikely that one will become an expert in all of these. With the varieties of domination that exist, the field of expertise becomes broader. It includes those with various historical and/or theoretical understandings of particular forms of domination, those who undergo domination, those who are linked in one way or another with those who undergo domination (friends of immigrants, relatives of homosexuals, etc.), and others who intersect with domination and struggle in their own ways.

In short, the shift from a view that accounts for politics in terms of a single site of oppression to a view that recognizes multiple sites of oppression is less likely to become oriented toward an avantgarde party. This does not mean that it is impossible for single-site proponents to resist the avantgardism or for multiple-site proponents to endorse it. However, their theoretical divergences lean them toward political divergences in the structure of resistance.

The democratic politics we have drawn from Rancière is of the second type. It does not reduce the idea of a police order to a single site of oppression, and, relatedly, rejects the idea of an avantgarde party. His concepts of the police order and active equality are of a piece theoretically. We might say that the central concept for Rancière is not that of exploitation but of domination, and, in keeping with this, define domination as the instantiation of the presupposition of inequality in a police order. This does not require him, of course, to abandon the claim that exploitation exists. Exploitation is a type of domination. But seen thus, it is a political rather than an economic concept. The wrong of exploitation is not that it extracts surplus value from the worker, but that it refuses to recognize the equality of the worker. The extraction of surplus value is a symptom of this refusal.

If we cannot bind Rancière's thought to the Marxist tradition, is there another one whose theoretical commitments lie closer? The suggestion here is that we might find Rancière's predecessors in the often neglected tradition of anarchism. Although a vibrant theoretical and practical force during the latter half of the nineteenth century, anarchism lay dormant throughout much of the twentieth century. During the 1960s and again more recently with the rise of the anti-globalization movement, anarchism has found new life. It has yet to be recognized, however, as an important theoretical tradition, on a par with Marxism. This has more than a little to do with its practitioners; anarchism has been more focused on action than on theory. However, misunderstandings and mischaracterizations of anarchism have played an important role in marginalizing anarchist thought. Anarchism is not simply a matter, as it has often been portrayed, of young, unshaven men in trench coats throwing bombs (although, to be fair, those young men and their bombs are also a part of the anarchist tradition). It is also a critique of domination and a practice of radical equality, one that is not foreign to Rancière's thought.[9] In drawing the contrast between exploitation and domination that we discussed a moment ago, the anarchist David Wieck writes:

> Basic to Marxists is the view that economic power is the key to a liberation of which the power of a party, the power of government, and the power of a specific class are (or are to be) instruments. Basic to anarchism is the opposing view that the abolition of domination and tyranny depends on their negation, in thought and when possible in action, in every form and at every step, from now on, progressively, by every individual and group, in movements of liberation as well as elsewhere, no matter the state of consciousness of entire social classes.[10]

At the outset, we should distinguish two views that have gone under the name of anarchism. The first is individualist anarchism, associated with thinkers like Max Stirner and Benjamin Tucker and closely aligned with (although, as we have seen, distinct from) Nozick's views presented in Chapter 1, which focuses on individual liberty. Individualist anarchists believe in the right of the individual to maximal liberty without interference by the state. It is often combined with a defense of free-market capitalism, capitalism unfettered. The view we will focus on here, which is the one most closely associated with the term anarchism, is what the greatest of the "classical" anarchists, Peter

Kropotkin, calls *communist anarchism*. Communist anarchism is the major tendency of anarchism, which Kropotkin defines generally in a famous passage as "the name given to a principle or theory of life and conduct under which society is conceived without government – harmony in such a society being obtained, not by submission to law, or by obedience to any authority, but by free agreements concluded between various groups, territorial and professional, freely constituted for the sake of production and consumption, as also for the satisfaction of the infinite variety of needs and aspirations of a civilized being."[11]

Under the rubric of communist anarchism would fall not only Kropotkin, but his predecessors William Godwin, Pierre-Joseph Proudhon, and Mikhail Bakunin. In addition, two of the more prominent recent thinkers who align themselves most closely with anarchist thought – Murray Bookchin and Colin Ward – are communist anarchists. How might we characterize the communist anarchist tradition, and what are the threads that tie it to the democratic politics we are articulating here? This is the question that will occupy us for the remainder of the chapter.

To approach this tradition, we can return to Kropotkin's definition of anarchism. It is intended to cover both individualist and communist anarchism. In order to do so, its central appeal is to the concept of liberty: free agreements, freely constituted. There is nothing here an individualist anarchist would dispute. What, then, would distinguish individualist from communist anarchism? For the communist anarchist, there is not only a commitment to liberty, but also and as deeply a commitment to equality. In discussing the morality of communist anarchism, Kropotkin writes,

> By proclaiming ourselves anarchists, we proclaim beforehand that we disavow any way of treating others in which we should not like them to treat us; that we will no longer tolerate the inequality that has allowed some among us to use their strength, their cunning or their ability after a fashion in which it would annoy us to have such qualities used against ourselves. Equality in all things, the synonym of equity, this is anarchism in very deed.[12]

What distinguishes individualist from communist anarchism is the latter's appeal to equality alongside liberty. As we have seen with Nozick, individualist thought does not value equality. Or, to put it in Sen's terms, the equality it values is that of liberty rather than opportunity, capabilities, resources, etc. The equality sought by communist anarchists (from here on, we will simply say *anarchists*) involves more than that of liberty. It also involves a recognition as equals and treatment that follows from that recognition: fundamentally, equal access alongside others, to building a meaningful life.

The dual commitment among anarchists to liberty and other forms of equality introduces a tension into their thought, a tension that does not appear for the individualist anarchist. For the latter, there is no difficulty in privileging liberty at the expense of other types of equality. For the anarchist, however, it is a problem that the privileging of liberty can result in inequalities in people's ability to construct meaningful lives. This difficulty is not only theoretical. In a world dominated by capitalism, it is precisely the ability of some people – those who have a part economically – to act with liberty that denies others the ability to flourish. Anarchists have, of course, long recognized this. It is why they seek to overthrow capitalism. But capitalism involves, among other things, the privileging of liberty vis-à-vis the goods that one owns. How, then, can anarchism reconcile its commitment to liberty with its commitment to other forms of equality? Is there a contradiction here, and if so, how ought it to be resolved?

In a study entitled *Classical Anarchism*, George Crowder argues that in order to understand these commitments, one has to grasp the general framework of nineteenth-century anarchism. He writes, "The central, defining argument of classical anarchism is that freedom is inviolable, that the State destroys freedom and ought therefore to be abolished, and that a stateless society characterized by freedom is a real possibility."[13] This argument is aligned with the definition of anarchism Kropotkin offers. It centers on liberty rather than any other form of equality. How, then, can one privilege liberty and still endorse equality? Crowder's view is that at the time the classical anarchists write, they have three corollary commitments that would dissolve the problem. First, they believe that freedom involves a commitment to objective morality, the kind of morality embodied in Kropotkin's Kantian view cited above. Second, on the basis of this view, they see the role of theoretical reflection to be that of radical political criticism. Third, they hold "the optimistic belief, generated by the rise of scientism, that moral truth, seen as inherent in the laws of nature, will eventually be the object of universal agreement."[14]

The web of these commitments buttresses a view that privileging liberty will lead naturally to an egalitarian society. The first commitment binds liberty to a particular moral view, the view that people should be treated as they would want to be treated. To be free is, as

Kant argued, to be subject to the moral law. Liberty is inseparable from a recognition of the equality of others. One might argue, however, that even if this is true, this does not mean that people will act in accordance with the moral law to which they are bound. The moral law is *normative*; it does not say that people will actually act in accordance with it. Nor does it say that people will even know what the moral law is.

For Kant this is not a difficulty, because he *defines* freedom as acting in accordance with the moral law. If one fails to act according to the dictates of the categorical imperative, it can be inferred that one is not free. Instead, one remains bound to the heteronomous desires of the empirical world, to one's animal desires. Freedom is what allows one to rise above animal instincts to the level of a rational creature. Conversely, the failure to act rationally – that is, morally – is a sign that one has not yet left the animal realm behind.

For the classical anarchists, the bond between liberty and the moral law need not be quite that tight. Rather, they can say that the exercise of freedom eventually leads to recognition of the moral law. This is the third commitment. If people are gradually becoming enlightened, and if there is a natural moral law that, like empirical laws, can be discovered and understood, then with enlightenment will come moral understanding and moral agreement. The nineteenth century is characterized by thinkers who are certain that humanity is coming to a point of enlightenment and emancipation, and that this point is at hand. (Think of Hegel and Marx.) The unfolding of a recognition of the moral law, of the idea that people should be treated equally, is a historical inevitability.

With this inevitability comes the second commitment, one that Crowder associates with the legacy of Jean-Jacques Rousseau: that the task of political thought is radical critique. The combination of the first two commitments leads to the conclusion that if people are allowed to act in accordance with liberty, they will eventually come to treat one another as equals. Further, since we are living at the culmination of the sciences, *eventually* means soon. Given this, there is no reason to place barriers to people's actions. Anything that constitutes a barrier to liberty must be abandoned. And, since the greatest barrier to liberty is the state, then it is the state first and foremost that must be dismantled.

This leads us back to the converging definitions of anarchism offered by both Kropotkin and Crowder. The difference between the (communist) anarchist and the individualist anarchist can be read here not straightforwardly as normative differences, differences about what should be valued. It is true that there are differences about what the moral law requires, but these differences are embedded in a larger framework that has to do with history and science, as well as morality. The anarchist is as devoted to liberty as the individualist anarchist. However, she believes that that devotion will lead elsewhere in the unfolding of practice.

The problem with this answer – and Crowder does not hesitate to point it out – is that we no longer hold these corollary commitments. "[T]he classical anarchist position rests on a teleological world-view which, although once central to Western thought, has now been widely repudiated."[15] Several factors have contributed to this repudiation. First, science is no longer associated with human perfection. Darwinian thought in particular has shown that evolutionary change is not equivalent to progress. Second, freedom is no longer seen as equivalent to submission to a moral law. Finally, although Crowder does not mention this, the political experience of the twentieth century has done much to dampen faith in human progress and the claims of utopian thought.

Crowder's view is an important perspective on the historical context in which classical anarchism – the anarchism of Godwin, Proudhon, Bakunin, and Kropotkin – developed and defended its ideas. It offers a coherent answer to the question of how anarchists can believe in liberty and yet endorse other forms of equality. It does so by reducing equality to liberty, showing that the exercise of liberty will itself lead to a society of equals. The cost of this coherence, though, is that of rendering anarchism anachronistic, tying it to a world-view whose grip no longer holds us. I want to suggest here that perhaps we should take another tack with regard to anarchism. Rather than holding it to be a coherent but anachronistic world-view, we should take it to be at once less coherent and more relevant.

That the classical anarchists are devoted to liberty is undeniable. However, they are devoted to equality as well, an equality that finds its expression in their thinking of themselves as communists. Their vision of an anarchist society is one of equals interacting on a voluntary basis, not of a free market defined simply by non-interference in market competition. We can see this vision in Proudhon's concept of mutualism, which envisions communities, preferably small ones, of people producing what is needed and trading with one another for everyone's advantage on the basis of equal exchange.

> Society must be thought of as a giant with a thousand arms, who carries on all industries and simultaneously produces all forms of wealth. Society is animated by a single consciousness, a single mind and a single will . . . In all circumstances this prodigious being remains true to itself, and one may say that each moment of its existence is equally productive.[16]

We can see it in Bakunin's critique of Marx's program in favor of spontaneous political activity from below, where he writes that, "the *doctrinaire revolutionaries*, whose objective is to overthrow existing governments and regimes so as to create their own dictatorship on their ruins, have never been and will never be enemies of the state . . . They are enemies only of existing governments because they want to take their place."[17] We can, if we like, read these ideas against the background Crowder offers us. But there is a more sophisticated reading, one that sees liberty and equality in an uneasy relationship with each other. That reading is perhaps best exemplified in Kropotkin's treatment of evolutionary theory, *Mutual Aid*.

Mutual Aid is written as a reply to Spencerian interpretations of Darwin, particularly those of Darwin's defender T. H. Huxley, which see every individual creature in competition with every other creature, both within and outside of the species, for survival. This interpretation is the basis for Social Darwinism, Herbert Spencer's view that a society ought to promote the survival of its fittest members through competition and allow those who are not fit to fall by the wayside. This view, although convergent with individualist anarchism, is anathema to the anarchism of the classical tradition. *Mutual Aid*, in an argument that has more recently been promoted by sociobiologists (without recognizing its roots in Kropotkin), argues that alongside competition, cooperation is an equally strong, if not stronger, factor in successful species reproduction and survival.

> [W]e may safely say that mutual aid is as much a law of animal life as mutual struggle, but that, as a factor of evolution, it most probably has a far greater importance, inasmuch as it favors the development of such habits as insure the maintenance and further development of the species, together with the greatest amount of welfare and enjoyment of life for the individual, with the least waste of energy.[18]

Kropotkin does not deny that there is intra-species competition, and he readily grants that there is inter-species competition. His view is that cooperation as an evolutionary factor has been neglected, and

88 *The Political Thought of Jacques Rancière*

that a proper interpretation of Darwinian thought requires it and should perhaps even privilege it.

> The strongest birds of prey are powerless in the face of the associations of our smallest bird pets. Even eagles – even the power and terrible booted eagle, and the martial eagle, which is strong enough to carry away a hare or a young antelope in its claws – are compelled to abandon their prey to bands of those beggars the kites, which give the eagle a regular chase as they as they see it in possession of a good prey.[19]

There is, then, within as well as across species, a dynamic interplay of cooperation and competition. They are in permanent tension. Sometimes cooperation prevails, sometimes competition. Neither can be irrevocably reduced to the other.

It is difficult to read this view of evolution in accordance with the framework Crowder has provided. Although Kropotkin claims that there can be, and indeed has been, moral progress, and that moral progress is toward a recognition of equality, he is not naïve about the relationship between liberty and equality. In a world characterized by competition as well as cooperation, free action can go in either a competitive or cooperative direction. Human history has shown us both. There may be moral progress, but we cannot rely on enlightenment about moral truths alone to create a society of equals.

This does not entail that there cannot be a utopian state of radical equality. Like Godwin, Proudhon, and Bakunin (or for that matter Marx) before him, Kropotkin has a strong element of utopianism to his thought. However, this utopianism is founded not only on moral or scientific but at least as much on *material* progress. It is the elimination of the motivation for competition – that is, scarcity – that can allow cooperation to prevail. The problem is not only that we have not yet achieved full moral enlightenment, but that the productive capacity of society has not been focused on securing well-being for its members.

> In our civilized societies we are rich. Why then are there many poor? Why this painful drudgery for the masses? Why, even to the best-paid workman, this uncertainty for the morrow, in the midst of all the wealth inherited from the past, and in spite of the power means of production, which could ensure comfort to all, in return for a few hours of daily toil? . . . It is because these few [the rich] prevent the remainder of men from producing the things they need, and force them to produce, not the necessaries of life for all, but whatever offers the greatest profit to the monopolists.[20]

In accordance with his endorsement of Darwinian thought, Kropotkin sees competition to be founded on a scarcity of material resources.

Kropotkin's more utopian moments rest not simply upon a nineteenth-century view of the relation of freedom, morality, and science, but also upon a view he shares with Marx and with many thinkers of the twentieth century that access to material security diminishes the motivation for competition. This does not mean that Kropotkin has a well-drawn view of the relation between liberty and equality. Things are quite otherwise in his thought. He indeed privileges both, although at the same time his views also display a recognition of their potential tension, particularly where people lack access to material sufficiency. Rather than a coherent view of the relation between liberty and equality that rests upon an untenable view of moral progress, Kropotkin offers a messier view of their relation based on a more credible view of the bond between material wealth and willingness to cooperate.

I would like to take things one step further. Rather than read anarchists as reducing equality to liberty, I propose that we do exactly the opposite: read them as reducing liberty to equality. I do so not in the name of interpretive accuracy, not as a claim that the anarchists really did privilege equality over liberty. As we have just seen, for Kropotkin the relation between the two is not well drawn. And what goes for Kropotkin goes for Bakunin and Proudhon as well, who were less theoretically sophisticated than Kropotkin. (We may leave Godwin aside here, whose views, while coherent, tend more toward the interpretation Crowder offers.) The point of reversing the relation between liberty and equality is political as much as it is hermeneutic. The anarchists are more relevant to us if we see them as privileging equality over liberty. They have more bearing on our contemporary context if we consider them to hold liberty to be a moment of equality. In other words, the proposal here is to offer a reading based upon an ambiguity in the anarchist tradition. This reading does not, I believe, violate anything central to anarchism. In fact, it captures many of its more powerful moments. In addition, it allows us to bring anarchism into contemporary political discussion.

I can only suggest the outlines of such a reading here. It rests on what is meant by reducing liberty to equality. It is here that the resources of Rancière's thought become relevant for a re-reading and renewing of the anarchist tradition. We have seen that anarchism, in contrast to Marxism and in accordance with Rancière's view, privileges political action from below rather than above. If Bakunin, for instance, is often too quick to trust the spontaneous instincts of the masses, it is as much because he distrusts hierarchy as because of his belief in the access to truth or justice by those who have no part. A commitment to action from below, then, can be founded on either of at least two other commitments. The first is that if one allows those who are governed to act in accordance with their natural orientation – in short, if one allows them liberty – they will naturally gravitate toward correct political action. This is the commitment that Crowder sees operating in the anarchist tradition. It underlies Bakunin's trust in spontaneous action, and no doubt is a moment of anarchist thought.

The alternative commitment one might make is to see action from below as stemming from a presupposition of equality. It is not because free action tends toward justice that action from below is to be privileged. It is because the only way to create equality is for people to act out of the presupposition of their equality with others. Equality, as we have seen, cannot be given, only taken. This commitment corresponds to Bakunin's distrust of hierarchies.

If, diverging from Crowder, we take this second route, what account do we give of the relationship between liberty and equality? Although a fuller normative discussion of the presupposition of equality will be given in the next chapter, we can at least address this issue here. Liberty is the freedom to act as one sees fit. Equality is the presupposition of equal intelligence, that each of us is capable of creating, alongside others, a meaningful life. One of the elements of a meaningful life is the ability to contribute to creating it. And that element itself has two aspects. First, if one cannot contribute to creating one's own life, it may turn out that the life one lives is not the life that one would have chosen. Assuming that I know as well as anyone else what a meaningful life is for me, then I had better have some input into the creation of that life. Otherwise, it might take a different path from the one I would have created. Second, if one cannot contribute to creating one's life, then in some sense it isn't *one's own* life that is being created. Without one's contribution, the life that is created is alienated from oneself. I become an audience to my life rather than a participant in it, and in that sense my life is no longer wholly mine. Sen captures this idea in emphasizing the importance of the capacities alongside functionings.

Both of these aspects require liberty. There must be liberty for one to create a life if that life is to go in the direction one seeks to take it. And there must be liberty if one's life is to be one's own. However, both these aspects of liberty are framed by a conception of equality: the equal intelligence required to create a meaningful life. This gives equality priority over liberty in two ways. The most obvious is that it gives equality *conceptual* priority. Liberty is conceived in terms of equality. It is the presupposition of equality that gives content to the idea of liberty. Equality also has *political* priority over liberty. Where there is a conflict between liberty and equality, equality trumps. This is the precise dividing line between individualist anarchism and the communist anarchism of the classical tradition. While individualist anarchism neglects equality in the name of liberty, communist anarchism subsumes liberty into equality, ensuring both its place and its limits by reference to equality. If we see things this way, we can coherently distinguish between individualist and communist anarchism, while still accounting for the importance liberty has played in both traditions.

Take, for instance, an example that might divide individualist from communist anarchists: the relation between a potential employer who is sexist and a female worker. Suppose there is an opening for a more advanced position and the female applies. She is told by the employer that she is incapable of doing the job and that he will not promote her. The individualist anarchist finds no problem with any aspect of this scenario. It may be that the employer is mistaken and that the woman may do as good a job as any male applicant. It may be abhorrent to the individualist anarchist that the employer is sexist. Politically, however, there is no injustice. The employer owns the company and is at liberty to do what he likes with it. The female is, of course, at liberty to quit the job and to tell others about the sexist practices of the employer. However, there is no political wrong that has been committed. A wrong would arise only if the employer were forced to promote the woman, because in that case the employer would have his liberty infringed.

For the anarchist of the classical tradition, there are several things wrong here, all of which create political openings. First, it is wrong that there is an employer who can decide the fate of his employee on an individual and non-cooperative basis. This, of course, is part of the larger anarchist rejection of capitalism. Second, that the woman is considered to be less than equally intelligent to men is wrong. Finally, that the woman's only recourse to criticism involves sacrificing the means of her livelihood is wrong. In the name of equality, political action to force the employer to give equal consideration in promotion, and, more radically, to end the private property relation that allows him these decisions in the first place, could all be justified. Otherwise put, his liberty cannot be justified at the expense of her equality.

It might be objected here, perhaps by a partisan of Nozick's thought, that true equality can be had only through a maximization of individual liberty. Recall his Kantian argument that to treat another as an autonomous human being is to accord her liberty in deciding the course of her life, and particularly in regard to the elements of distributive justice in her life. In the example, if the employer is coerced regarding his property, then he is not being treated as an autonomous being. That failure, according to Nozick, *just is* the failure to see someone as an equal being. The reasoning here is strict. According to Kant, a person can be treated either as an autonomous being – a being of reason – or as a heteronomous one – a being driven by desire. Moreover, a free being is a being of reason. Autonomy → reason → freedom. To violate a person's autonomy, then, is to treat that person as an unfree being, as a being incapable (at least at that moment or in that way) of reason. Moreover, in that violation, one is taking *oneself* to be a being of reason. It is because one knows better than the other what ought to be done that one intervenes on the autonomy of the other. The upshot is that one treats oneself as a being of reason and the other as a being of less-than-reason. The violation of autonomy, then, amounts to a presupposition of inequality.

This argument contains two untenable assumptions. First, it assumes a strict division between reason and desire. The strictness of that division, common at the time of Kant's writing, has been abandoned in more recent thought. It is not that there is no difference between reason and desire. Rather, the assumption of a chasm between them has come under question; reason and desire are now considered intertwined aspects of a human being. The implication of this is that if one cannot divide strictly between reason and desire, one also cannot divide strictly between treating someone as an autonomous being and treating her as less than autonomous. Judging when someone is being treated as less than autonomous becomes a judgment call, subject to criteria other than solely that of liberty. To put the point another way, treating someone equally is not reducible to respecting her liberty.

The second untenable assumption is that the exercise of one person's liberty does not affect the autonomy of someone else. Nozick tries to circumvent this problem in his approach by considering liberty only as a matter of distributive justice. In the example, there is no injustice done to the woman because nothing that she owns was taken from her without her consent. On the other hand, if the employer had been forced to promote the woman – or, according to anarchist dictates, had had his property appropriated for collective decision-making – then he would have suffered an injustice. He would not be able to do what he wants with what he owns, i.e. his business. This view works, if it does, only on the assumption that liberty can be reduced to the possession and exchange of goods. The weakness of this view is manifest. The exercise of one's autonomy is not simply a matter of economic exchange. It involves the creation and enactment of various life projects. It is entirely possible to use, say, one's economic power to violate the autonomy of another's life projects. An employer who discriminates against women is surely violating her autonomy in a recognizably Kantian sense: he is treating her as less than an autonomous being, a creature of reason. Once again, equality cannot be reduced to respecting liberty.

None of this amounts to a proof that liberty can be reduced to or conceptually framed by equality. What we have offered here is no more than suggestive. We have sought to give at least an initial plausibility to the primacy of equality in order to be able to distinguish individualist from communist anarchism and in turn to show that the tradition of communist anarchism is not simply the historical relic that it is on Crowder's interpretation. The picture we are painting of anarchism ascribes to it two central theoretical commitments, both of which are brought forward in Rancière's thought: a critique of domination in all its forms and an embrace of active equality. These are, of course, inseparable in ways discussed in Chapter 2.

The first commitment, a critique of domination in all its forms, is exemplified in the passage from David Wieck cited above. While Marxism centers its political critique on economic relations, anarchism operates with a non-reductionist view of politics. Domination, in contrast to exploitation, is a plastic concept. Elsewhere, I have used the terms *strategic* and *tactical* to distinguish between these two approaches.[21] A strategic political philosophy takes is that there is a single explainer, a single node, to which politics can be reduced. Therefore, the project of political justice is to form an overall strategy that addresses that node. By contrast, a tactical political philosophy rejects the idea that there can be a single node that, when changed, corrects the injustices of all social relationships. Domination is multifarious and irreducible, even though there may be certain forms of domination that are more egregious, more pervasive, or that ramify out into other forms. It must be addressed by a multitude of struggles across a variety of fronts. Marxism is strategic; anarchism is tactical.

This point has often been obscured in the treatment of anarchism. It is often thought that both Marxism and anarchism are strategic political philosophies, the former focusing on economic relations, the latter on the state. On this view, for instance, Bakunin's critique of Marx's project of a dictatorship of the proletariat is centered on the worry that it would retain a state apparatus, when it is the state that is the problem. Bakunin's position is subtler than that. Bakunin opposes hierarchies in all their forms, including that of the state. Anarchist critiques often focus on the state, since it is a particularly powerful form of hierarchy and a particularly effective supporter of domination. But it is because of the state's relation to domination and hierarchy that the state is a problem for anarchists, not simply because it is the state.

The multiple character of anarchist critiques of domination can be seen as early as Bakunin's *God and the State*. This text contains not only a critique of organized religion and of the state, but also of science as practiced by those who see its mission as that of offering a final account of life and how it should be lived. Science, he argues, has been used to govern people by reducing them to general and abstract categories to be manipulated by the scientific method. "Scientific abstraction is their God, living and real individuals are their victims, and they are consecrated and licensed sacrificers."[22] Science as it is practiced treats human beings as general categories rather than living individuals. While it might be appropriate to appeal to science, then, in order to learn about the world, the use of science as a method of governing human beings is oppressive. "The government of science and of men of science . . . cannot fail to be impotent, ridiculous, inhuman, cruel, oppressive, exploiting, maleficent."[23]

Bakunin's critique of science is not divorced from his critiques of the state and of organized religion. We should not see them, however, as a triangle, with the state at its apex. What the practice of science, organized religion, and the state exhibit is a mutually reinforcing set of hierarchical relations among human beings. Each tries to govern humans in league with the others rather than recognizing the possibility of voluntary *self*-governance. Later, in her essay on anarchism, Emma Goldman offers a similar non-reductionist tripartite critique. "Religion, the dominion of the human mind; Property, the dominion of human needs; and Government, the dominion of human conduct, represent the stronghold of man's enslavement and all the horrors it entails."[24]

This non-reductionist orientation is found in contemporary anarchism as well. Colin Ward, perhaps the most prominent figure in recent British anarchism, analyzes in his book *Anarchy in Action* how domination works in schools, factories, housing, city planning, and elsewhere. He notes that, "There is no final struggle, only a series of partisan struggles on a variety of fronts."[25] Although he privileges the state as a site of power, he does not hold the strategic view that destroying the state will in turn liberate people from what oppresses them. The state is emblematic of hierarchy rather than being its sole and defining source. Even when the state coordinates dominations occurring in other areas, eliminating the state will not lead automatically to the collapse of those other dominations.

What is common to anarchism, then, is the claim that injustice is a matter of domination, of hierarchy. To put the point another way, injustice is a matter of people being treated unequally. However, as anarchists are quick to note, the cure for this is not for people to be treated equally by those who have treated them unequally. Anarchists do not call for passive equality. Such a call would be both naïve and self-defeating. It is naïve to think that those with power over others or those who benefit from a hierarchical power relationship will relinquish it without struggle. History constantly proves otherwise. Moreover, even if the impetus for equality comes from those at the top, the fact that it is they who offer equality implies that the power relationship still exists. Equality must be created by those who have been denied it. This is the other side of the anarchist coin, corresponding to its critique of domination: resistance must come from below, from the people, the demos.

It is perhaps the most constant theme in anarchist thought. Kropotkin writes, "our studies of the preparatory stages of all revolutions brings us to the conclusion that not a single revolution has originated in parliaments or in any other representative assembly. *It all began with the people.*"[26] This is not simply a historical observation. It is a political necessity.

> [W]e must recognize, and loudly proclaim, that everyone, whatever his grade in the old society . . . has, before everything else, the right to live, and that society is bound to share amongst all, without exception, the means of existence it has at its disposal . . . This cannot be brought about by Acts of Parliament, but only by taking immediate and effective possession of all that is necessary to ensure the well-being of all;

this is the only really scientific way of going to work, the only way which can be understood and desired by the mass of people.[27]

This theme finds echoes in both earlier and later anarchist thought. It is in Proudhon's call for a mutualism developed voluntarily from below and Bakunin's trust in the spontaneous action of the masses. The organizational structure most often called for by the classical anarchists is federalism: the coming together of local units in a voluntary structure that has no administrative power above and beyond that granted by the units themselves.[28] It appears later in the thought of both Murray Bookchin and Colin Ward. Ward suggests that "we have to build networks instead of pyramids . . . Anarchism does not demand the changing of labels on the layers, it doesn't want different people on top, it wants *us* to clamber out from underneath."[29] (Compare this statement with Rancière's position that a democratic politics seeks to undermine police orders, not change or modify them.) Bookchin in turn calls attention to the importance of the process of change standing alongside its outcome. "[T]here *can be no separation of the revolutionary process from the revolutionary goal.* A society whose fundamental aim is self-administration in all facets of life can be achieved only by self-activity."[30]

Bookchin's emphasis on process has become a staple of contemporary anarchist practice. In contrast to Marxist practice, which allots decision-making to an avantgarde party, anarchism holds to the idea that everyone involved in a group must have a say in the decisions taken by that group. (The anti-globalization movement of the 1990s was strongly oriented toward this way of proceeding.) The motivating idea is that the society that one wants to have emerge must already be reflected in forms of political resistance. "*A society based on self-administration must be achieved by means of self-administration.*"[31] Otherwise, when one replaces the hierarchies one is struggling against with other hierarchies, there is no subversion of the police order, simply a new police order. Bakunin, as we have seen, criticized Marx on precisely this point: the dictatorship of the proletariat becomes, in the end, just another dictatorship. The state does not wither away; it must be dissolved from below.

We should note here in passing that the importance of process to anarchist practice has led to what is perhaps its most central conundrum: whether decision-making must be strictly by consensus or can at times be by majority (or super-majority) vote. In anarchist and anarchist-oriented conferences that I have attended, perhaps no issue of process is so often discussed. Those in favor of consensus argue that any other model will inevitably leave some people's interests out. Unless *everyone* signs on to a particular decision, those who have not ratified it become de facto unequal to the majority. They must abide by a decision with which they disagree. Others argue that the consensus model is too unwieldy, particularly in larger associations. To insist upon full consensus for each decision is not a matter of respecting the equality of all participants; it is instead a recipe for paralysis. The question facing anarchists in this area, one that has not yet been resolved, is how to make decisions in an orderly and efficient manner while at the same time respecting the equality of each participant in the decision procedure. While Bookchin's insistence upon process is generally ratified, the character of that process has still to be adequately constructed. (In Chapter 4, we will return to the idea of group norms, although the discussion there will not resolve this debate.)

The picture of anarchism drawn in the previous pages is one where equality rather than liberty is primary. Oppression is a matter of domination, of the denial of equality in various aspects of social life. Resistance to domination must come from the dominated themselves, as well as those in solidarity with them, rather than from the dominators. To allow, as Rancière would put it, the part that has a part to grant equality to the part that does not undercuts the very project of equality. This does not mean that liberty has no role to play. Rather, respect for liberty is a central requirement of the recognition of equality. We ought not, however, to misinterpret the centrality of liberty for its primacy.

Anarchism has been the most dogged proponent of a democratic politics, in both theory and practice, that the West has witnessed. Perhaps this is one of the reasons it has been so violently opposed and so rigorously suppressed over the course of its history. Unlike the passive equality of the liberal tradition or the avantgarde approach of Marxism, anarchism privileges the presupposition of equality of everyone with everyone else. If the reading of anarchism offered here is adequate, then even where anarchists seem to focus on liberty rather than equality, it is because of their belief in the equal respect each person should enjoy. On this reading, the democratic politics whose framework Rancière has drawn is continuous with the anarchist tradition. It is a continuity he seems willing to embrace. In a recent work he writes, "Democracy means this above all: anarchic 'government,' founded on nothing other than the absence of all title to govern."[32] Rancière does not align himself openly with the anarchist tradition, or for that matter with any other one. He seeks instead to discover what characterizes movements worthy of the name *democratic*. However, his orientation is not foreign to that of anarchist thought and practice.

Although Rancière's work is closely aligned with that of anarchism, we should be wary of applying the term to his work without qualification. The democratic politics we have drawn from his work is a rigorous thinking of what I take to be the most productive reading of anarchism. It cannot, however, be taken to be representative of anarchism as a whole. There are at least two reasons for this. First, the phrase *anarchism as a whole* is misleading. If what has been said here is right, anarchist thought is often in tension with itself. This is largely because its theoretical tradition has not thought through important issues, such as the relation of liberty to equality. It would be a mistake to reject the reading Crowder offers of classic anarchism. The threads he isolates – the commitment to objective morality, the emphasis on political critique, the faith in scientific progress – are not illusory. They are as much a part of the anarchist tradition as the critique of domination and the privileging of equality we have emphasized here. Moreover, the privileging of liberty that rests upon those threads exists side by side with that of equality, and sometimes in tension with it. If the democratic politics of the previous chapter is unswervingly a matter of equality, the anarchist tradition has been less clear, at least in theory if not in practice, about the role played by equality. This is what has given individualist anarchism the opening to see itself as part of the same tradition as the communist anarchism of the most classical and contemporary anarchists.

The other reason Rancière's democratic politics keeps a certain distance from anarchism is the element of utopianism that creeps into anarchist thought. Crowder, as we saw, founded this utopianism in the convergence of morality and science. By contrast, Kropotkin seems to found its possibility as much in material as in spiritual progress. He explicitly rejects the term *utopia*, with its connotations of dreamy idealism.

> The anarchist writers consider, moreover, that their conception is not a utopia, constructed on the *a priori* method, after a few desiderata have been taken as postulates. It is derived, they maintain, from an *analysis of tendencies* that are at work already . . . The progress of modern technics . . . the growing spirit of independence, and the rapid spread of free initiative and free understanding in all branches of activity . . . are steadily reinforcing the no-government tendency.[33]

Proudhon, Bakunin, and Kropotkin, in common with other nineteenth-century thinkers like Hegel and Marx, are convinced that they live in a time characterized by the convergence of important historical forces. Material and ideological tendencies have led to a moment in which the possibility, if not the imminence, of a just and proper society is at hand. This enthusiasm is not limited to the nineteenth century. Bookchin's writings during the 1960s and 1970s display a faith in the ability of the youth movements of the time to create a utopian society. "On a scale unprecedented in American history, millions of people are shedding their commitment to the society in which they live. They no longer believe in its claims. They no longer respect its symbols. The no longer accept its goals, and, most significantly, they refuse almost intuitively to live by its institutional and social codes."[34]

Rancière, writing in the more sober 1980s, 1990s, and 2000s, has no patience for utopian thinking. He rejects even the possibility of institutionalizing democratic politics, a point we will return to in the final chapter. Democratic politics, for him, is a rare event, one that does not lead to a final state of justice but perhaps only to better conditions in a police order. Democratic politics, as we have seen, lies in the expression of equality rather than in the end-state it achieves. In this, Rancière's thought resembles that of Colin Ward, who warns against utopian thinking in anarchist movements. Ward writes, in words that could have been penned by Rancière, "The choice between libertarian and authoritarian solutions is not a once-and-for-all cataclysmic struggle, it is a series of running engagements, most of them never concluded, which occur, and have occured, throughout history."[35]

Anarchism, then, is neither the ground out of which Rancière's, democratic politics emerges, nor is his thought simply a repetition of the work of anarchists who precede him. Rather, anarchism constitutes a historical trajectory out of which the thought and practice of a democratic politics should be read. It is the neglected alternative of recent Western thought and practice, the other path which progressive thought abandoned and to which, I believe, it should return. Rancière's accomplishment is to offer a framework in which this progressive thought can achieve greater clarity and rigor. In contrast to many of the strains of the Marxist tradition, it offers a democratic politics for our time, a democratic politics that focuses on the demos.

Having seen what a democratic politics looks like, and having drawn the historical tradition out of which it can be read, we must ask now about the normative framework of this politics. It is not

enough to know what a democratic politics is. Where does the justification for such a politics lie? What is compelling about it? Why
ought we to embrace and act upon the presupposition of equality that
it expresses?

Notes

1. Louis Althusser et al. (eds), *Lire le Capital*, Paris: Maspero, 1965. The
   article was later translated into English as "The concept of 'critique' and
   the 'critique of political economy'" in *Ideology, Method, and Marx:
   Essays from* Economy and Society, ed. Ali Rattansi. London: Routledge,
   1989. It is interesting to compare the dry, academic prose of this early
   piece with the impassioned clarity of many of his later political works.
2. May '68 was a famous student-led uprising that occurred over the
   months of May and June, 1968. It influenced, in different ways, a generation of French thinkers, including Foucault, Deleuze, Derrida, and
   others. For a fascinating account of the events of May and their long-
   term effects, see the fascinating study by Kristin Ross, *May '68 and its
   Afterlives* (Chicago: University of Chicago Press, 2002), where she views
   the events from a broadly Rancièrean perspective.
3. Jacques Rancière, *La Leçon d'Althusser*. Paris: Gallimard, 1974, p. 33.
4. Jacques Rancière, *The Philosopher and His Poor*. tr. John Drury,
   Corinne Oster, and Andrew Parker. Durham, NC: Duke University
   Press, 2004 (or. pub. 1983), p. 118.
5. His historical study of this period is *Nights of Labor: The Worker's
   Dream in Nineteenth-Century France*, tr. John Drury. Philadelphia:
   Temple University Press, 1989 (or. pub. 1981).
6. For the dispute between Bakunin and Marx, see Paul Thomas, *Karl
   Marx and the Anarchists* (London: Routledge & Kegan Paul, 1980),
   esp. pp. 300–29, and James Joll, *The Anarchists* (2nd ed., Cambridge,
   MA: Harvard University Press, 1980), esp. pp. 79–96.
7. Quoted in Joll's *The Anarchists*, p. 92.
8. Karl Marx and Friedrich Engels, *The Communist Manifesto*, in
   Lawrence Simon, *Karl Marx: Selected Writings*. Indianapolis: Hackett,
   1994 (essay or. pub. 1848), p. 158.
9. In what follows in this chapter, one might, if one chooses, see a response
   to Alain Badiou's charge that Rancière's view is, ultimately, apolitical.
   See Badiou's "Rancière and Apolitics," in *Metapolitics*. tr. Jason Barker.
   London: Verso, 2005 (or. pub. 1998), pp. 114–23.
10. David Wieck, "The Negativity of Anarchism," in *Reinventing Anarchy*,
    ed. Howard Ehrlich, Carol Ehrlich, David DeLeon, and Glenda Morris.
    London: Routledge and Kegan Paul, 1977 (essay or. pub. 1975), p. 141.
11. "Anarchism" (article for *Encyclopedia Britannica*), in Peter Kropotkin,
    The Conquest of Bread and Other Writings, ed. Marshall S. Shatz.

Cambridge: Cambridge University Press, 1995 (essay or. pub. 1910), p. 233.

12. Peter Kropotkin, "Anarchist Morality," in *Kroptokin's Revolutionary Pamphlets: A Collection of Writings*, ed. Roger N. Baldwin. New York: Dover Publications, Inc., 1927 (or. pub. 1909), p. 99.

13. George Crowder, *Classical Anarchism: The Political Thought of Godwin, Proudhon, Bakunin, and Kropotkin*. Oxford: Clarendon Press, 1991, p. 4.

14. Crowder, *Classical Anarchism*, p. 4.

15. Crowder, *Classical Anarchism*, p. 171.

16. From *On the Political Capacity of the Working Class*, cited in *Selected Writings of P.-J. Proudhon*, ed. Stewart Edwards, tr. Elizabeth Fraser. New York: Doubleday and Co., 1969 (or. pub. 1865), p. 65.

17. Michael Bakunin, *Statism and Anarchy*, tr. and ed. Marshall S. Shatz. Cambridge: Cambridge University Press, 1990, p. 137.

18. Peter Kropotkin, *Mutual Aid: A Factor of Evolution*, ed. Paul Avrich. New York: New York University Press, 1972 (or. pub. 1902), pp. 30–1.

19. Kropotkin, *Mutual Aid*, pp. 44–5.

20. Kropotkin, *The Conquest of Bread*, pp. 12–13.

21. Todd May, *The Political Philosophy of Poststructuralist Anarchism*. University Park, PA: Penn State Press, 1994, esp. Chapter 1.

22. Michael Bakunin, *God and the State*. New York: Dover Publications, 1970 (or. pub. 1882), p. 56.

23. Bakunin, *God and the State*, p. 55.

24. Emma Goldman, "Anarchism," in *Anarchism and Other Essays*. New York: Dover Publications, 1969 (or. 3rd ed. published 1917), p. 53.

25. Colin Ward, *Anarchy in Action*. London: Freedom Press, 1988.

26. "Modern Science and Anarchism," in *Kropotkin's Revolutionary Pamphlets*, p. 190.

27. Kropotkin *The Conquest of Bread*, pp. 28–9.

28. Murray Bookchin discusses the federal character of the anarchist movement in late nineteenth and early twentieth century Spain in his book *The Spanish Anarchists: The Heroic Years 1868–1936*. New York: Free Life Editions, 1977.

29. Ward, *Anarchy in Action*, p. 22.

30. Murray Bookchin, "Post-Scarcity Anarchism," in *Post-Scarcity Anarchism*, 3rd ed. Edinburgh: AK Press, 2004 (or. pub. 1970), p. 11.

31. Murray Bookchin, "The Forms of Freedom," in *Post-Scarcity Anarchism*, p. 104.

32. Jacques Rancière, *La Haine de la démocratie*. Paris: La fabrique editions, 2005, p. 48.

33. Goldman, "Anarchism," p. 234.

34. Bookchin, "Post-Scarcity Anarchism," p. 13.

35. Ward, *Anarchy in Action*, p. 136.

CHAPTER 4

The Normative Framework of Democratic Politics

Among the various conflicts between the left and the right, one issue seems never in dispute: the right gets morality. The right claims it; the left cedes it. In the U.S., the term *moral values*, closely aligned with its subsidiary *family values*, figures prominently in conservative discourse. Conservatives see a certain decline in the U.S. that stems from its disengagement with morality and moral values, and seek a return to them in order to stem that decline. The left, broadly defined, often takes issue with the specific values endorsed by this discourse – opposition to equal rights for gays and women, for instance – and with the direction in which conservative discourse leads, but never with the framework of the discourse itself.

There is a belief on the left, common to both progressive theorists and activists, that the discourse of morality itself contains a certain conservative element. Morality is at once dictatorial and provincial. This can be seen particularly in discussions around multiculturalism. The attempt by progressives to promote multicultural studies at universities is often defended on the basis of a denial of morality rather than on the basis of its moral worth. Instead of an appeal to the value of respect for and tolerance of other cultures and viewpoints, the defense of multiculturalism relies on the absence of any common values. The universalist claims put forward by morality, it is said, fail to recognize the diversity that characterizes different people's moral lives. The argument runs roughly like this: since there are no universal moral values, no set of values can claim ultimate superiority over any other; therefore, people should be exposed to a diversity of moral views.[1]

The appearance of the word *should* in the conclusion might pique our interest. If there are no universal moral values, one is tempted to ask, what is the origin of this *should*? However, at issue for the moment is not the coherence of the argument but its basis in the denial of universality, one of the central characteristics of morality. This same denial occurs in a more subtle way in recent French thought.

There is a reluctance among prominent French philosophers associated with poststructuralism to engage in moral discourse. This reluctance appears in several ways. For Michel Foucault, it appears mostly as a silence in his own discourse. Foucault shies away from what Gilles Deleuze once called, in conversation with him, "the indignity of speaking for others."[2] For Foucault, it is important that those who are engaged in political struggle dictate the terms of that struggle. He rejects the idea of a "universal intellectual" whose role is to tell people where their ultimate truth lies and how to achieve it. In fact, his historical approach seeks to discredit the project of assuming such a role. "All my analyses are against the idea of universal necessities in human existence."[3]

For others, like Deleuze, morality is to be criticized on a Nietzschean basis. Morality assumes a transcendent figure that looms over us – God or Reason or the Good – judging us from on high. Instead of morality, we are better off embracing a Spinozist ethics, seeking not to conform to pre-given transcendent values but to experiment with modes of existence immanent to the world we inhabit. "Ethics, which is to say, a typology of immanent modes of existence, replaces Morality, which always refers existence to transcendent values."[4]

Still others, for instance Jacques Derrida and Emmanuel Levinas, take a different tack. For them, it is not morality itself that is to be jettisoned, but traditional moral discourse. There is an obligation to the other, an obligation that is rigorous, unrelenting, and can be described as nothing other than moral. However, that obligation does not arise out of a form of moral discourse. To appeal to such a discourse already subsumes the other into one's own cognitive categories, reducing the other to one's own framework, and thus betrays the otherness of the other.

These are nothing more than brief gestures at complex philosophical positions. Even in these gestures, however, we can see normative elements at work. In Foucault, the resistance to speaking for others is a normative one. There is something wrong with representing another's good to him or her, an "indignity" in Deleuze's apt term. And for Deleuze himself, the project of morality reveals what Nietzsche would call a *reactive* consciousness. Rather than exploring the immanent character of our world, to see what it is capable of yielding, morality's project is one of submission to a transcendent other, an other that rejects rather than embraces this world. The turn from morality to ethics, then, has normative implications.

At issue here is not the term *morality*. We may call these matters what we like. However, we are inescapably entrenched in an arena of normative judgment, of judgments of the better and the worse that are supposed, in one way or another, either to bind people to or discourage them from something. What is *intolerable* (to use a term Foucault was fond of) about speaking in the name of others or judging human life by transcendent values is that these practices violate our ability to choose for ourselves or restrict us unnecessarily from experiments in our living. This intolerability is ineluctably normative. It submits us, Derrida and Levinas notwithstanding, to the realm of linguistic judgment and reasons, to the realm, if not of principles, than at least of principled evaluation and discussion.

To put the point another way, the positions endorsed by these thinkers, if they are not bound to transcendence or to absolutist morality (and they are not), are bound to something akin to what has been called universality. But we must be clear about what universality means. Because universality has been so long tied to transcendence, it is not an easy matter to prise them apart. The traditional view has it that what makes values or duties universal is that they arise from a source that is either common to all humanity, like Reason, or to which all humanity is subject, like God. The thought is that if there is a common source, then everyone is bound by its dictates. Inasmuch as I am a creature of Reason or subject to God's will, whatever it is that Reason or God's will tells me I should do or be or value becomes my immediate duty to do or be or value. And since we are all such creatures, we are all so bound. Universality is founded in the transcendence that founds morality.

However, the claim of universality need not be tied to transcendence. It can be more philosophically pedestrian. When Foucault calls certain practices or arrangements of power intolerable, he need not appeal to God or Reason or the Good. He can say instead that there are good reasons to oppose those practices, in a more everyday sense of the term *reasons*. Normalization is intolerable, not because it violates a transcendent moral requirement, but because it makes us into blind conformists and binds our bodies to capitalist production. Inasmuch as these consequences of normalization are intolerable, so is normalization.

Now one might be tempted to argue here that criticisms of blind conformism and capitalist production themselves need the support of reasons, and that this process of reasoned support will be unending unless it is grounded in some form of transcendence. Either there is a stopping point for reasons, a place they come to rest, or there is an infinite regress of reasons, which means they are ultimately ungrounded. And if there is to be a stopping point, it must be in a solid foundation, in something that transcends our usual experience.

We need not follow this path, however. The fact that we cannot defend a normative claim all the way down does not mean that it is arbitrary or ungrounded. It simply means that we no longer live in a world where philosophical foundationalism is an option. We no longer inhabit the philosophical space inhabited by Descartes or Kant or even the more recent philosopher Edmund Husserl, where it would be possible for reasons to come to rest in a foundation that supports the entire edifice. This is the lesson of much of Ludwig Wittgenstein's work. "Nothing we do," he writes, "can be defended absolutely and finally. But only by reference to something else that is not questioned. I.e. no reason can be given why you should act (or should have acted) *like this*, except that by doing so you bring about such and such a situation, which again has to be an aim you *accept*."[5]

Philosophically, we must abandon the search for certainty in morality, just as long ago we abandoned the search for certainty in science. There is no ultimate grounding for either. Their claims are subject to the best reasons one can give in defense of those claims. But if we abandon the search for certainty in morality, we must also abandon the critique of morality that sees it as a search for certainty. This is the lesson for progressives who seek to think in the tradition of recent French thought. What both moral conservatives and progressives share – something that has led conservatives to embrace morality and progressives to reject it – is a common and mistaken assumption about morality: that its dictates and values are grounded in an unshakeable foundation of God or Reason or the Good. This assumption reinforces the further mistaken view that moral judgment is necessarily an enterprise of applying a narrow and provincial set of values – for instance, from the Bible or Western civilization – to all peoples and cultures.

If we think of universality instead as a matter of reasons one gives people for the things they believe one ought to value or do, then the discourse that has flown under the banner of morality need no longer be grounded in anything transcendent, and therefore need no longer be a matter of fear for progressives. The kinds of reason we call *moral* and the kinds of values we call *moral* can be thought of as matters of normative judgment without requiring us to move backwards philosophically. To say that something is wrong or intolerable is to say that there are good reasons that ultimately weigh against doing it. Progressives need not, and should not, abandon the battlefield of morality. Instead, it ought to be claimed for progressive thought and action.

For Rancière's democratic politics, the project of an ethics or a morality is even more urgent. The concept of domination plays a central role in the intersection of democratic politics with anarchism. As we saw in the previous chapter, domination, in contrast to exploitation, is a plastic concept. It does not have a natural site (ex. the economy), and can refer to a number of different types of power arrangements. In order to sort out which power arrangements are dominating and which are not, we need a value by which to judge them. Which power arrangements are those of domination? Those that involve or reinforce inequality. Therefore, there is an inescapably normative element to Rancière's concept of equality. If there are normative implications to the work of thinkers like Foucault and Deleuze, in Rancière's work the normativity is not implicit. One of his central concepts is normative. It operates in a way that would be difficult to describe in terms other than ethical or moral. The question then is what to make of equality as a normative term. How does it function in the discourse of democratic politics?

The presupposition of equality plays a dual ethical role in Rancière's democratic politics. The first is in regard to those *against* whom one is pressing the presupposition, the second in regard to those *alongside* whom one is pressing it. Put in Rancière's terms, the presupposition of equality has an ethical role to play regarding those who have a part and a different role to play with those who have no part. We must look at each in turn, because the presupposition of equality functions differently in the two cases.

When one acts out of the presupposition of equality, particularly in societies that think of themselves as democratic, one confronts the elites, those who have a part, with a contradiction. The contradiction does not belong to the political actors but to the elites. It is a contradiction that is usually veiled; political action brings it out into the open. On the one hand, elites in a nominally democratic society believe in equality. It is woven deeply into the belief structure of such societies that everyone is equal. Whether this belief is a purely normative matter – that everyone should be treated equally – or more ontologically grounded – that people are indeed equal in whatever sense is important for politics – is irrelevant. What is relevant is that the belief in equality is held. It is an ideological given in societies that call themselves democratic that they are founded on the equality of their citizens.

On the other hand, there is, alongside this, a commitment to inequality. That commitment is usually not doxastic; it is not a belief in inequality per se. Rather, it involves a commitment to the hierarchies and dominations of a given police order. To believe that a given hierarchical police order is just or proper is implicitly to be committed to the inequality of speaking beings. It is to believe that the distribution of roles, which places some in the role of speaking for others, ordering them, exploiting them, in short dominating them, is at least ethically permissible and indeed ethically proper. To be sure, this commitment is rarely made explicit in the thinking of the elites. It is instead a commitment that follows from their other, consciously held, commitments.[6] (Which is not to say that there is no one among the elites that explicitly holds the belief in the inequality of those who have no part, only that in nominally democratic societies this is rarer.)

In the United States, for instance, the belief in equality is deeply held. Everyone is born equal, and therefore everyone is capable of succeeding if given the opportunity – which generally means if no obstacles, such as racial preference, are put in their way. On the other hand, people are not treated equally, and not simply through racial preference. Managers treat workers as though they are less intelligent and less capable; men often treat women in much the same way. The structure of work, of public politics, of family relations, of class relations, function on the basis of presumed inequalities that are often unspoken and even unrecognized.

This is the contradiction. On the one hand, those who have a part, at least in nominally democratic societies, hold to a principle of equality. On the other hand, by ratifying a hierarchical police order, they hold to a principle of inequality. If one were to follow a traditional Marxist line, one might be tempted to say that the former commitment is ideological while the latter is real. The commitment to equality is no more than a formal, legal commitment that serves only to conceal the real relations of inequality that lie behind or beneath it. Rancière rejects this way of thinking about the contradiction. He suggests instead that we take both sides of the contradiction seriously, and that one of the roles of political action – that is, acting out of the presupposition of equality – is to bring them out into the open.

To see this more clearly, we can return to the example of the French tailors' strike discussed in Chapter 2. There Rancière offers a historical example of the making explicit of a contradiction. The preamble to the French Charter of 1830 stated that all French people are equal before the law. However, in practice workers were treated unequally, and in a variety of ways. In fact, Rancière quotes a public prosecutor saying that, "Everything which the Law has done against press license and against political associations would be lost if *workers* were daily to be given a picture of their position, by comparison with a more elevated class of men in society, by repeated assurances that they are *men just like those others*, and that they have a right to enjoy the same things."[7] While one might read this as a more explicit rejection of equality by the public prosecutor, the prosecutor would in all likelihood also have acknowledged the preamble to the 1830 Charter, without recognizing the contradiction involved.

What does political action do in this case? It forces the contradiction to be recognized. "If Monsieur Persil or Monseiur Schwartz is right to say what he says and do what he does, the preamble of the Charter must be deleted. It should read: the French people are not equal. If, by contrast, [the preamble] is upheld, then Monsieur Persil or Monsieur Schwartz must speak or act differently." Here is the core of the ethical situation. It lies not in the violation of a principle that is inescapable, or in acting contrary to universal reason, but in contradicting *one's own* stated principles.

Approaching things this way, taking the contradiction seriously, has an effect that is missed if we revert to the traditional Marxist tactic of denouncing official pronouncements of equality as merely ideological. If we take the second tack, then the political message is that people's beliefs are radically mistaken. They are simply fooling themselves. The elites are fooling themselves to their own benefit and the people are fooling themselves to the benefit of those elites. It makes people out to be dupes.

Alternatively, if we take the contradiction seriously, the political message is not that people are dupes, but that there is a tension in their world that needs to be resolved. It is often a tension between what is said and what is done, although it can be a tension between different sayings or between different doings. In any case, to argue that there is a tension in one's world is not to find him or her to be a dupe. All of us live with such tensions, and part of our growth is to discover and resolve them. What makes a particular tension political is that it is a tension around equality. To tell someone among the part that has no part that they are not living the equality that their society has endorsed as intrinsic to their character is not to find them to be blind or incompetent. It is instead to invite them to live that equality, to act out of the presupposition that is said to be their birthright.

If we are to abandon foundationalism in ethics, we can do no better than this by way of ethical critique. The reason for this is complex, but its outlines can be given here.[8] If we reject the idea that there have to be ethical principles to which everyone is committed by virtue of being human, or rational, or children of God, then we can only engage in ethical critique utilizing principles that are actually held (or, alternatively, principles that are not held but follow from other principles that are actually held). We must rely, as Wittgenstein says, "on something else that is not questioned."

This can happen in at least two ways. First, one can criticize someone who does not hold certain ethical principles precisely for the failure to hold them. This is a dogmatic position, but one that is sometimes inescapable. It occurs at the point where ethical dialogue breaks off, and force usually begins. For instance, faced with someone who persists in claiming, in the face of all evidence, that Jews or Palestinians or African Americans are inferior to other races (assuming one can make sense of the concept of a *race*), ethical discussion has nowhere to go. One must choose either to allow the person to act on a prejudice that violates one's own principles or to stop them. Although this situation can arise, and is highlighted in certain publicly visible cases like abortion, I suspect it is more exceptional than the second way ethical critique can occur.

This second way involves internal contradiction rather than external critique. We have already seen it in the example Rancière provides. Rather than chastising someone for failing to recognize an ethical principle, one shows instead that the principle is recognized, but that it conflicts with other principles one also holds or that one is implicitly committed to by virtue of other commitments or actions. Here the failure is one of consistency: the person criticized is in contradiction with himself or herself.

Rancière points out that, in the case of the French Charter, there are two possibilities open to the prosecutor: to deny the principle of equality, or to act in ways consistent with the principle. (It should probably be noted in passing that there is, logically, a third possibility: the prosecutor can commit himself to inconsistency. However, the problems with this position are manifest; it leads to incoherence.) In the passage where Rancière discusses this case, one may suspect a bit of irony at work. Who, one might ask, would seriously deny the principle of equality, and thus ask for a revision of the preamble? And, indeed, the possibility may sound strange to many of us. However, it is a possibility that must be taken seriously at the philosophical level. In the absence of foundationalism, nothing commits one to choose one way rather than another. There is nothing inconsistent about choosing against equality, nothing in fact that requires the acceptance of any particular ethical principle. There is no transcendence to appeal to that would resolve once and for all on which side of the contradiction one must fall. The prosecutor can, without violating any dictates of logic, accept a principle of inequality. If he does, then anyone opposing him is forced to return to the first position: external critique.

This does not mean that it is arbitrary which principle will be accepted. In a nominally democratic society, there is a strong motivation to embrace some kind of principle of equality. And it is the point of political action in Rancière's sense to widen the scope of that embrace by showing its contradiction with much of current social and mainstream political practice. Political action provides, in a single gesture, a proof of equality to those who have no part and of contradiction to those who have a part. The second aspect of that gesture is at once political and ethical, and, as Rancière recognizes, offers no guarantee of success. "Whereas Jacotot's critique confined the verification of equality within the continually recreated relationship between a wish to say and a wish to hear, such a verification becomes 'social', causes equality to have a real social effect, only when it mobilizes an *obligation* to hear."[9] The suggestion here is that that obligation is mobilized through the staging of a contradiction.

Rancière often speaks of this contradiction in terms of the appearance of two worlds. "The essence of politics is the manifestation of dissensus, as the presence of two worlds in one."[10] This idea can be taken in both a political and an ethical sense. In the political sense, it refers to the appearance of a political subject, the emergence of a subjectification, that we have seen in Chapter 2 and will return to below. But the idea of an appearance of two worlds also has an ethical significance, one that is implicit in Rancière's work. The action of democratic politics brings an ethical contradiction around equality into the open. It displays two worlds: one where there is equality and one where there is not. The first world may be primarily linguistic in character, although it doesn't have to be. Nevertheless, it is a lived world just as the other one is.

These lived worlds are not merely cognitive in character. We have seen that for Rancière politics is not just a matter of beliefs and actions, it is also a matter of sensibility. Every police arrangement involves a partition of the sensible, a partition that leaves some people unequal to others. This inequality is not only a matter of belief. In fact, it need not be a matter of belief at all. One who lives with a sense of inferiority toward others experiences the world in a different way. It is a more fragile, more threatening world, one that is more opaque and less yielding. To introduce another world into this one, a world of equality, is to sense the world differently. This sensibility lends one an aura of empowerment, in which the world opens itself at the same time that one feels a greater sense of one's own capacities. This is one reason why political movements generate such a sense of excitement among their participants. The sense of lived helplessness of the police order is thrown off, a future opens up, and the world appears in brighter hues than before.

Before the emergence of a democratic politics, there is only one world. There is no lived tension, because the contradiction between those who are considered equals and those who are not remains unaddressed. There may be two sensibilities – a sensibility of the elites, with its world of possibilities and hope; and a sensibility of the part that has not part (or the parts that have no part), of a world more ominous and less pliant. It is only with the emergence of a democratic politics, a people acting out of the presupposition of their equality, that the tension between the two, and therefore the emergence of two worlds in tension, can appear. This is why Rancière, criticizing those who think the rise of modern politics, especially Nazism, introduced aesthetics into politics, responds that, "There never has been any 'aestheticization' of politics in the modern age because politics is aesthetic in principle."[11] Democratic politics introduces another sensibility, another world, into the lived world of the police order. Moreover, it introduces that sensibility retroactively. The equality of democratic politics, as we saw in the second chapter, will be introduced as something preceding its emergence in the democratic movement itself.

These worlds are not symmetrical though. It is not just that there happen to be two worlds, each of equal normative weight. Rancière writes, "The 'people' that is the subject of democracy . . . is the supplementary part, in relation to any counting of parts of the population that makes it possible to identify 'the part of those who have no part' [*le compte des incomptés*] with the whole of the community."[12] In what sense might the part that has no part identify with the whole of the community? My suggestion is that that identification is normative.

It is not that the part that has no part is the *real* community, as though what has been before was either fake or ideological. To hold that would be to neglect the constitutive tension that Rancière ascribes to democratic politics. The police order is as real as the democratic politics that challenges it.

The identification with the whole of the community concerns its ethical fabric. By acting out of the presupposition of equality, those involved in a democratic politics are acting in the name of a value that the whole of any nominally democratic society endorses. If, as we have seen, the struggle of contemporary liberal political theory is to articulate what type of equality is the relevant one for distributive justice, this is because there is a prior embrace of equality as a value. What a democratic politics, a politics of the demos, accomplishes is the realization of that value. If there is a tension between the stated value of equality in a nominally democratic society and its ongoing practices, a democratic politics sides with the value. It seeks, through its action, to align those practices with that value. And in doing so, it identifies with the whole of the community, with that to which the whole of the community sees itself as committed.

There is a complex relation, then, between the dissensus of a democratic politics and the society in which that dissensus occurs. A dissensus creates two worlds, but these are not non-communicating worlds. They are bound through a common normative structure. If the worlds were entirely distinct, if they had no point of contact, every political struggle would be a fight to the death. Every democratic politics would reduce itself to a struggle between two competing visions, only one of which could prevail. There could be no democratic politics that wasn't entirely revolutionary. This is not how a democratic politics operates. The bond that holds these two worlds together, and that can make the dissensus compelling even to those who are not participating in it, is ethical. There is at least one common normative element in any nominally democratic society that binds those who struggle and those against whom they struggle. This common element – a commitment to equality – means that dissensus can impress itself without necessarily resorting to violence (a point we will return to below), that a democratic politics can be compelling not only to those who struggle but to those who do not.

This common normative element is the universality without transcendence that underpins a democratic politics. Rancière writes that, "Politics . . . is the art of the local and singular construction of cases of universality."[13] We can see why this is. A democratic politics is not an exercise in theory. It is an exercise in confronting one sensibility, with its normative weave, against another. The confronting world, the world of democratic politics, acts in the name of an equality that is supposedly part of the weave of the confronted world, but is not. In essence, a politics of equality confronts a contradiction with a universality. A politics of gay rights, for instance, confronts a world that preaches but does not live equality with a *singular construction* of the universality of equality. Here, now, in this demonstration, in this wedding ceremony, in this act of love, the universality of equality is constructed, over and against the police order that at once posits and denies equality.

So far, we have been discussing the ethical relation of equality in regard to those against whom one is pressing a democratic politics. This is one side of the ethical coin. The other side is internal to politics; it concerns the part that has no part itself. The part that has no part does not have to be confronted with a contradiction. By presupposing its own equality, it has already, in the moment it acts, overcome any contradiction between a belief in equality and an implicit commitment to inequality. That is already over the moment politics begins. However, there is an ethical character to the bond created by political action that has its own integrity. Rancière rarely discusses it, but it can be derived from his characterization of the bond itself.

What political action does, Rancière tells us, is create a subject where there was none before. As Foucault and others have taught us, the supposition of a subject of the type liberal theory envisions lying beneath its actions and decisions is deeply problematic. Rancière does not deny this. We have seen that in his thought there is no political subject that first exists and then decides to act. A political subject – a collective political subject – is created through action, and specifically through action that expresses the presupposition of equality. It does not pre-exist its own activity.

Before political action, there are simply diverse individuals acting in accordance with the roles allotted to them by the police order. People are classified and, through their behavior if not in their beliefs, accept their classifications. To engage in the presupposition of equality is at once to reject one's classifications – democratic politics declassifies – and to create oneself as a subject: an actor with no name other than that of being equal. "By subjectification I mean the production through a series of actions of an instance and a capacity for enunciation not previously identifiable within a given field of experience, whose identification is of a pair with of the reconfiguration of the field of experience." The proletariat is not the name of a group that pre-exists political action. Before such action there are only workers. The proletariat is the name of a group that emerges when it assumes the name *proletariat*, along with the internal unity and equality that that name implies. "Politics does not happen just because the poor oppose the rich. One must say rather that politics (that is, the interruption of the simple effects of domination by the rich) causes the poor to exist as an entity."

What is the ethical character of this subjectification? What happens among those who form a democratic community in action? Rancière is suggestive but only suggestive here. I would like to follow hints provided in two passages in his essay "The Uses of Democracy." He tells us that, "Democracy is the community of sharing, in both senses of the term: a membership in a single world which can only be expressed in adversarial terms, and a coming together which can only occur in conflict."[14] And he ends the essay with the words, "The test of democracy must ever be in democracy's own image: versatile, sporadic – and founded on trust."[15] Sharing (the original French term is *partage*) and trust (*confiant*).[16] It is these ideas that we must follow if we are to grasp the ethical nature of political action, that is, the appearance of a democratic community.

We might initially suspect that the ethical character of a democratic community would be broadly Kantian. People would treat others with equal respect, as ends rather than merely means, and as co-participants in a kingdom of ends. If we were to follow this line, then we would find Rancière offering us a third Kantianism in contrast to Rawls' and Nozick's Kant. Rawls' Kant is a Kant of pure rationality, a Kant who chooses in accordance reason and not inclination. Nozick's Kant is a Kant of autonomy, a Kant who opposes interference in people's creating their life. Rancière's Kant is one of equal respect. Kant writes of the kingdom of ends, "For rational beings all stand under the *law* that each of them should treat himself and all others, *never merely as a means*, but always *at the same time as an end in himself*. But by doing so there arises a systematic union of rational beings under common objective laws – that is, a kingdom."[17]

We might take Rancière to be proposing a democratic political reading of Kant. If the kingdom of ends is conceived as one of equality, where each is presupposed equal to the others and where each acts out of that presupposed equality, then what Kant is pointing toward is not simply a collection of autonomous individuals in Nozick's sense or rational individuals in Rawls' sense, but instead a collective subject. Equality would not be attached to individuals but would rather be the ether of the community itself. In this sense, Rancière's conception of a kingdom of ends would reject the individualism of the liberal tradition out of which Nozick and Rawls (and indeed Kant himself) writes in favor of a more interpersonal view of equality and of the kingdom that arises from its presupposition.

This reading would not be entirely mistaken. However, the Kantian flavor of this characterization misses something important. It is too cognitive. It remains embedded in the language of obligation and duty. While it is true that, considered as obligations, Kantian morality has captured the internal ethical character of a democratic community, we should suspect that that character itself is not exhausted by the obligations assumed by its participants. There is something more.

We can approach that excess by recognizing that the concepts of sharing and trust do not lend themselves to an entirely cognitive approach. Sharing and trust are based not on reason – or at least not solely on reason – but on an affective bond that eludes the formal morality of a Kantian (or, for that matter, utilitarian) approach. Kant makes a strict division between acting for the sake of duty and acting out of inclination. We have already seen this.

> [T]o preserve one's life is a duty, and besides this every one has also an immediate inclination to do so. But on account of this the often anxious precautions taken by the greater part of mankind for this purpose have no inner worth, and the maxim of their action is without moral content. They protect their lives *in conformity with duty*, but not *from the motive of duty*.

The non-cognitive aspect of sharing and trust efface such a distinction between duty and inclination.

This is a lesson that pre-dates Rancière's work. It has been taught to us by feminist theorists of ethics, from Carol Gilligan onwards. In describing many women's approach to ethics, Gilligan tell us, "Sensitivity to the needs of others and the assumption of responsibility for taking care lead women to attend to voices other than their own and to include in their judgment other points of view. Women's moral weakness, manifest in an apparent confusion of judgment, is thus inseparable from women's moral strength, an overriding concern with relationships and responsibilities."[18] The Western tradition of ethical thought – and Kant is perhaps its best exemplar – has been characterized by a privileging of the rational, the cognitive element in our relations with others. It has devalued sensitivity and the bonds that often lie at the ground of our connection to others. It has ignored what Hume – an exception to the tradition – calls *sympathy*: "No quality of human nature is more remarkable, both in itself and in its consequences, than that propensity we have to sympathize with others, and to receive by communication their inclinations and sentiments, however different from, or even contrary to our own."[19]

Ethics need not be solely a matter of duties and obligations. Principles can be lived as connections with others rather than simply as obligations to them. When one is confronting an adversary, when those who have no part act politically against those who do, then the appeal to duties and obligations is more pertinent. There is no meaningful connection to those who are dominating one, or who are gaining by domination. But the creation of a collective subject through political action is the creation of internal connections, and the ethical character of that subject would be incompletely described if one did not recognize them. Sharing and trust are markers of a set of connections that arise through the political process of subjectification. They indicate a willingness to expose oneself to those alongside whom struggle takes place.

To share is to offer part of what one has to another or to others, to make a part of oneself available in a way that does not require an equal return. It is, in that sense, asymmetrical. Sharing can be contrasted with exchange, in which the act of giving is coupled with the expectation of return. And because it is distinguished from exchange, sharing carries with it a political significance. In an economy governed by expectations of personal gain (expectations that play into the hands of those who are best situated to obtain personal gain), sharing is a deviant relationship. It stakes out an alternative to the police order of a capitalist society. We will return to this point in the next chapter.

Trust, concomitantly asymmetrical, is an affective relationship of vulnerability before and with the other. Like sharing, it constitutes a rejection of exchange relationships. Trust can arise only in a context where one considers others as more than vehicles for personal gain and, in addition, as similarly motivated. Trust, then, both relies on and contributes to the presupposition of equality within a process of subjectification.

Sharing and trust do not exclude a more cognitive set of obligations. Rather, the affective and the cognitive are woven together. In a political movement, not everyone is motivated by trust or inclined to share, and no one is all the time. There is also a role to be played by the cognitive recognition, against what one is often taught, that those others with whom one is engaging in political action are indeed one's equals. If Kant is not exhaustive in understanding the ethical character of political action, neither is he irrelevant. But we must bear in mind that the ethical character of political action is not the same among those engaged in the action as it is among those who are confronted by it. In the latter case, a contradiction of principles is central to the ethics of politics; in the former case, the principles in play are at times grasped cognitively, at times lived affectively, and at times both.

In political action, the tapestry of this weaving together of cognitive and affective elements around the presupposition of equality has a name, although that name is rarely reflected upon. It is a name we invoked in the Chapter 2, but without a full understanding of its character: *solidarity*. Political solidarity is nothing other than the operation of the presupposition of equality internal to the collective subject of political action. It arises in the ethical character of that collective subject, a subject that itself arises only on the basis of its action. When one joins a picket line, or speaks publicly about the oppression of the Palestinians or the Tibetans or the Chechnyans, or attends a meeting whose goal is to organize around issues of fair housing, or brings one's bicycle to a ride with Critical Mass, one is not – if one is engaged in democratic politics – doing so from a position above or outside those alongside whom one struggles. Rather, one joins the creation of a political subject (which does not mean sacrificing one's own being to it). One acts, in concert with others, on the presupposition of the equality of any and every speaking being.

And here is where the justificatory character of the ethics of political action lies. It cannot lie, as we have seen, in an ethical framework that possesses an ultimate foundation. It lies instead in a principle – the presupposition of equality – that can ground and justify political action only to the extent to which it is accepted by those alongside whom *and* against whom one struggles. It is, in that sense, an optional ethical principle. But, as we have also seen, this does not mean that it is an arbitrary one. In our world, the presupposition of equality is embedded deep within the ethical framework of most societies. Even when it is honored in the breach, it remains honored. Political action consists in narrowing the breach.

Here, however, we may be faced with a dilemma. It involves the relation between the politics of equality and its ethics. Rancière seems to be holding two positions, one political and one ethical, that are in tension. On the one hand, his view of politics may be seen as descriptive. A democratic politics exists under certain conditions: when people act out of the presupposition of equality. This is a characterization of democratic politics; it has no normative element to it. On the other hand, he seems to give a normative privilege to equality. Equality is a good thing; there ought to be more of it. Where equality is denied, that should be changed. There seems to be an ambivalence here between political description and normative evaluation.

This, by itself, does not present any difficulty. The difficulty lies with the role of the concept of equality. If Rancière is providing mere political description, there is no reason why anyone should have to act upon it. He is noting a particular political phenomenon – the formation of a democratic politics. He is neither commending nor privileging it. This would be a strange reading of his work. It misses the critically engaged character of terms like *police*, *equality*, and *democracy*. However, if he is involved in a more normative project – if he wants not only to describe but also to commend a democratic politics – then is he not denying in action the equality that lies at the basis of this politics?

How might this be? To commend equality is to commend that people act in accordance with a democratic politics. For Rancière, commending equality cannot be, at least first and foremost, a demand upon the elites to provide or ensure it. That would be a return to passive equality. A normative privileging of equality would seem to be addressed to the demos, the part that has no part. It would be a call to action. If the *demos*, acting in accordance with the presupposition of its own equality, places a demand upon the elites, that would be fine. But Rancière's own discourse does not operate at that level. It does not ask anything of the part that has a part. Its addressee is the *demos*.

But to call the *demos* to action places Rancière's discourse in the position of the avantgarde discussed in the last chapter. What distinguishes Rancière's more anarchist approach from that of avantgarde Marxism lies in its recognition that it is the people rather than appointed or elected leaders from whom the decisions about action must arise. The presupposition of equality rejects the division into leaders and followers, at least at a theoretical level. (It may be that there are those who, for reasons perhaps of time or interest, *choose* to be followers in a democratic politics.) If Rancière's discourse is calling upon people to engage in a democratic politics, he seems to be returning to the relation between intellectuals and the people that he rejects in his break with Althusser. This is a relation of inequality rather than the equality that is the central theme of his political thought.

Here is the dilemma. If Rancière is offering only a description of democratic politics, then it has no normative force, and the critical element that it seems to possess is lost. Alternatively, if the framework of his thought is not merely descriptive but also normative, as this chapter argues it is, then it undercuts the very equality he endorses.

The position Rancière carves out is more subtle than the dilemma would make it appear. Put baldly, there are two claims that he endorses, and one that he does not. The claims he does endorse are that first, a democratic politics is a politics of equality; and second, it is wrong to deny the equality of others. The claim he does not endorse is the one that seems to bridge those two: that the demos is obliged to act in the name of its own equality. In seeing how this is so, we will also see the distinction between politics and ethics in the conception of a democratic politics.

If Rancière were to hold that people *ought* to engage in democratic politics, that they were somehow obliged to do so, then he would indeed be violating the strictures of his own thought. But he need not do so, even though he criticizes inequality and recognizes that inequality is only really overturned through a democratic politics. To criticize inequality is to hold that the elites have committed a wrong against the *demos* by holding them to be unequal. The elites, those who have a part, have failed (at least in action) to ratify the assumption of equal intelligence which we discussed in Chapter 2. One might be tempted to conclude from the existence of this wrong that the elites owe something to the demos, to the part that has no part. Those who benefit from the oppression of gays, or the Burmese people, or Jews, owe them at least the recognition of equality, if not more. The problem, as we have seen, is that addressing the debt to the beneficiaries of inequality places the oppressed in the position of a passive equality, which in essence is a position of inequality.

If the oppressed, the *demos*, acts in the name of its own equality, then this problem is addressed. However, this does not *oblige* people to act in the name of their own equality. This is the key point. The solution to inequality is not, and cannot be, an obligation placed upon those who are capable of solving it. To do so would be, in American parlance, to blame the victim. You are the one who has been wronged, and you are further wrong if you do not address that wrong. It would also be a violation of the discourse of democratic politics.

This does not mean that one cannot address the members of the *demos* and point out an inequality they are living without recognizing it. One is not barred from claiming an unrecognized inequality. What is implied is that such a project would be educational in nature but does not introduce any obligation for the members of the *demos* to emancipate themselves. The claim, "You are not being recognized as equals" does not entail, "You should act to achieve recognition as equals."

The coherent position to take, and on my reading it is Rancière's position, is not that the part that has no part is obliged to engage in a democratic politics, but that when there is a democratic politics, it ought to be endorsed and supported by others. When a democratic politics is in play, when a wrong is being staged, then one is called upon to recognize and address that wrong, whether or not one is in the elite, whether or not one is the beneficiary of the inequality that constitutes the wrong that is being confronted. There is no normative obligation to create a democratic politics, but the existence of a democratic politics introduces norms into a situation where they did not previously exist. Just as a democratic politics creates a subjectivity that did not pre-exist it, it also creates normative obligations for those occupying that situation that did not exist before the emergence of the politics.

And here lies the distinction between politics and ethics. Democratic politics is not simply founded on an ethics. The situation is not one in which there is a founding principle – equality – from which a democratic politics is deduced or on the basis of which it is constructed. The relationship is more complex. On the one hand, equality provides an ethical justification for democratic politics. In that sense, it would seem that the politics is grounded in the ethics. On the other hand, equality does not demand the creation of a democratic politics. Rather, it is the existence of a democratic politics that obliges the recognition of equality. That recognition, as we have seen, is addressed to both those outside and inside the democratic movement: outside in the form of a contradiction, inside in the form of sharing and trust (although the latter, as the reference to feminist ethics shows, do not lend themselves to the form of moral obligations or duties).

To put the point another way, it is not the discourse on democratic politics – Rancière's discourse or the discourse of this book – that creates certain ethical obligations; it is the existence of the politics itself. "Politics occurs by reason of a single universal that takes the specific shape of a wrong. Wrong institutes a singular universal, a polemical universal, by tying the presentation of equality, as the part of those who have no part, to the conflict between parts of society."[20] This position, unlike the one presumed by the dilemma, is in accordance with the equality at the core of Rancière's thought and the anarchist approach discussed in Chapter 3.

One might think that this position implies that before the emergence of a democratic politics, there is no ethical wrong committed by the part that has a part toward the part that does not. This would be mistaken. Where there is an inequality, there is a wrong. Where one is aware of the inequality, particularly if one is benefiting from it, one is obliged to address it. In a society in which there is no democratic politics – a society that is, in the terms used earlier, a single world rather than two worlds, a society without dissensus – there are certainly still inequalities. These are lived as different sensibilities, but they may not be recognized as inequalities, as tensions between what one endorses through one's words and what one endorses through one's practices. In this case, there is a wrong but not yet an obligation to address that wrong. One cannot be obliged to change something that one has not been in a position to recognize. What a democratic politics accomplishes is to introduce obligation by manifesting or staging the wrong.

Further, there does not have to be, at least in principle, a democratic politics in order to create this obligation. One can imagine a theorist or commentator pointing out an inequality that has not been recognized, and addressing her discourse to the beneficiaries of that inequality. This is the status of Rawls' or Sen's discourse. It is, indeed, the structure of most discourses in the tradition of passive equality. The circulation of such discourses, inasmuch as they are justified, could itself introduce obligations. However, we must recognize two things. First, as a practical matter, it is difficult for theory to have political effects without its converging with a political movement. The elites do not read political tracts and then decide to introduce equality. It is only in combination with the pressure of a political struggle that theory takes hold of practice. Second, changes that would result solely or primarily from a discourse of passive equality lack the advantages of a democratic politics. They might be ameliorative, but they would not be emancipatory.

There is another difficulty the normative framework of democratic politics must face. It concerns the political status of the values it promotes, in this case that of equality. The difficulty arises most trenchantly in reference to Foucault's thought, so we will place it in that context. In the second chapter, the question arose of the relation of the concept of equality to history. We saw that for Foucault and Kuhn, historical analysis undercuts a naïve view of the chronological or thematic continuity of certain concepts. My argument there was that continuity could be undercut for some concepts only by holding other concepts as continuous. There is a holism to the kinds of historicism Foucault and Kuhn endorse that allows one to interrogate any particular concept as to its historical or thematic unity, but only by holding other concepts (or other aspects of the same concept) constant.

One of the distinctions between Foucault's work and that of Kuhn is in their view of power, and that is where the normative difficulty for the concept of equality may arise. Kuhn's view of the operation of power in scientific practice, while revolutionary in its application to science, remains within a traditional view of what power itself is and does. Power lies in the ability of some people to control or repress what other people do. What makes Kuhn's work unsettling, even to this day, is that he displays the operation of power in the epistemic field of science, which many think immune to power. Foucault's works, particularly his genealogical works, go one step further. He seeks not only to show the operation of power within epistemic disciplines, but also offers a novel view of how power works, one that has implications for the normative status of equality.[21]

In Foucault's view, power is not simply repressive. It is also creative. Power does not just stop things from happening, like the state stopping a person from conducting her life by putting her in jail; It also makes people into the kinds of beings they are. It creates them. We tend to think of power as a possession that one can use in order to make someone do something, or prevent them from doing something. Foucault does not deny that this type of power exists, but it is, particularly in the modern world, secondary to the type of power that molds people and their behavior: a positive, creative power rather than a negative, repressive one. Power does not simply operate to stop people from being what they would otherwise be, as though there were some essence or pre-existence to people's desires that power can only intervene on afterwards. Power helps shape those desires in the first place, and even more deeply it helps to shape us into the kind of people that would have those desires.

Moreover, this type of power works not only through people's intentions, but also at the level of practices themselves. When people engage in their daily practices, whether they be familial, vocational, political, athletic, or otherwise, they are also engaged in creating and sustaining relations of power. "Relations of power are not in a position of exteriority with relation to other types of relationships (economic processes, knowledge relationships, sexual relations) but are immanent in the latter."[22] Power, then, is not to be found in the place most people traditionally look for it: in the state. Rather, it is dispersed among the various practices that form the ether of our lives.

There is a third aspect of power that results from these two. If power is immanent to practices and is creative as well as repressive, then it is also something that operates outside most people's awareness and even their control. "Power is not something that is acquired, seized, or shared, something that one holds on to or allows to slip away; power is exercised from innumerable points, in the interstices of nonegalitarian and mobile relations."[23] This is because if power is immanent to practices, it is widespread rather than concentrated in the hands of particular groups of people. Further, if it creates as well as represses, then those involved in power are as much its products as its sources. Therefore, they are already being molded by the very relations of power that they deploy.

We might illustrate this operation of power by reference to the first volume of Foucault's history of sexuality, where Foucault sketches a history of the emergence of contemporary sexuality, a genealogy of sexuality that traces the dispersed origins of its current arrangement. In Foucault's view, the idea, prevalent in the late 1960s and early 1970s, that we have liberated ourselves from the sexual repression of previous generations is mistaken. The story he criticizes is that until recently sex was hidden, an area of our lives that remained shrouded in silence, but now people can speak openly about it. Light has been cast upon the darkness in which sex was forced to hide. This view of sexual liberation is mistaken, not so much because sex is still hidden but because it was never hidden. To the contrary, "since the end of the sixteenth century, the 'putting into discourse of sex,' far from undergoing a process of restriction, on the contrary has been subjected to a mechanism of increasing incitement."[24]

We can see here the Foucauldian view of power at work. The question he asks about our sexuality is not one of how it was repressed, but rather of what kinds of "incitement" it was subject to. How has it been made to be what it is? What is the historical process that molded us into the sexual beings we are now? Foucault's own view in the first volume of *The History of Sexuality* is only suggestive, and in later volumes he turns his attention to earlier forms of sexuality, those of ancient Greece and Rome. However, we can still get an idea of the trajectory he saw his work moving in.

Briefly, before the counter-reformation, sex was simply a matter of what one did. Sexual transgressions were behavioral transgressions. During the seventeenth and eighteenth centuries, however, it was not simply acts but also desires that came to have theological significance. One confessed not only what one did but also what one thought about doing, what one desired, what one imagined. Desire, rather than acts, became the centerpiece around which confession revolved. At the same time, economic changes were forcing nations to consider the size and deployment of their populations. Population studies, with their rates of births and deaths, became matters of state, and with them a concern for the health and reproductive practices of national populations. This concerned merged with the new confessional and gave sexuality a pride of place, if an ambivalent and morally charged one, that it had not enjoyed previously.

These practices, and others like them – for instance, the emergence of psychiatry – combined to create a focus on sex that saw it as the key to who people are. Identity came to be defined largely by sexual desires and attitudes. As people were subjected to these practices, they came to see themselves – and to that extent to become – beings defined by their sexuality. "[T]wo processes emerge, one always conditioning the other: we demand that sex speak the truth . . . and we demand that it tell us our truth,"[25] or, in a more concise formulation, "Sex, the explanation for everything."[26]

Foucault isolates four figures created by this sexuality: the hysterical woman, who will become a particular concern of Freud's; the masturbating child, who requires constant attention and intervention in order to prevent him from going astray; the Malthusian couple, who are the ideal couple to which all should aspire; and, of course, the perverse adult, whose emblem is the homosexual. We can see the legacy of this history at work today particularly in the last figure. The homosexual is the person defined by his or her sexuality. Homosexuals are primarily and inescapably sexual beings, at least in the view of those around them. And inasmuch as they appropriate this legacy, they turn themselves into beings defined by their own sexuality. We have seen this appropriation not only in rise of Queer Studies, but more generally in the self-imposed ghettoization into gay communities that many gays have chosen. This ghettoization is certainly understandable in the face of ongoing discrimination, but at the same time it reinforces the legacy of sexuality that Foucault traces.

The question that must be confronted here does not concern a particular Foucauldian genealogy. It concerns the politically charged character of normative evaluation. Suppose our practices are suffused with power. Suppose that the epistemic judgments we make are inseparable from (although, as Foucault often emphasizes, not reducible to) relations of power. Would not the same hold true for our ethical and moral judgments? Would not the normative force of Rancière's appeal to equality be in part the product of power relations that constitute who we are? And if so, might that appeal be another, if subtler, form of "the indignity of speaking for others"? Put another way, might Rancière's discourse be another discourse of power, one that is all the more dangerous for being unaware of its own political roots? What separates his discourse from Catholic discourse on sex, or its confessional legacy in Freud and psychoanalysis?

We cannot answer this question by appealing to the distinction between politics and ethics we made a moment ago. It would be inadequate to say that the *demos* is not obliged to engage in democratic politics, and that therefore the concept of equality presents no difficulty here. What is at issue is not what people are or are not asked to do. Rather, it is the normative framework within which politics is being thought. Democratic politics holds movements that presuppose equality to be a good thing, just as Catholicism holds confession of one's desires to be a good thing. However, if Foucault is right, the latter is not a good thing. So what about democratic politics? If democratic politics is justified by the norm of equality, what, in the face of Foucault's view of power, justifies equality?

To approach this question, we must first recognize that the concept of equality is not immune to genealogical critique. It would be possible to trace the origins of the concept and its normative force. Any practice, any concept, can be investigated genealogically. But what does it mean to say this? What follows from the fact that one can trace the dispersed roots, practices, and power relations out of which something emerges? To trace a genealogy, to find the dispersed origins and follow the creative power relations connected to or emerging from a practice or a term, is not necessarily to find that practice or that term to be politically suspect. If one knew in advance that, for instance, the received conception of sexuality were problematic, one would not have to bother tracing its history. It could be declared politically suspect at the outset; history would be irrelevant.

It is only through a genealogical investigation that one discovers *whether or not* a practice or a term embodies a deleterious power relation. The fact that power relations are inscribed into our practices does not, by itself, entail that we ought to abandon them. As Foucault tells us, "[R]elations of power are not something bad in themselves, from which one must free oneself. I don't believe there can be a society without relations of power, if you understand them as a means by which individuals try to conduct, to determine the behavior of others."[27]

There is a distinction to be drawn between power relations, which are pervasive, and domination, relations of power that we ought to abandon. This distinction has not always been clear, and the failure to maintain it can lead to misplaced visions of utopia. In anarchist thought, for instance, we have seen that there is, particularly in its nineteenth-century incarnation, a tendency toward an optimism about human beings that hopes for the dissolution of relations of power. However, if power relations are inescapable, then political thought must become more nuanced. It is not that wherever there are power relations there is domination. Rather, we must say that wherever there are power relations there is the possibility of domination. If power relations are everywhere, and if power is inseparable from domination, then our situation is politically hopeless. There is nothing to be done, since we cannot escape from power, and therefore from domination. On the other hand, if we separate power from domination, we find ourselves at once opposed to hopelessness and to an uncritical utopianism that believes we can shed not only current forms of domination but its very possibility. Foucault remarks of his work, "My point is not that everything is bad, but that everything is dangerous, which is not exactly the same thing. If everything is dangerous, then we always have something to do. So my position leads not to apathy but to a hyper- and pessimistic activism."[28]

There are two lessons to be drawn from these reflections. The first is both epistemic and political. It has a bearing not only on the normative framework of equality but on any claim or belief or epistemic practice. We cannot know in advance of reflection whether a claim or a belief is politically suspect. There is no philosophical procedure that tells us a priori whether the ways we are thinking or the beliefs that arise from those ways of thinking are complicit with forms of domination. Nothing is immune from genealogical investigation. Nothing is protected in advance; nothing is condemned in advance. We must always be ready to reflect on the history and character of our practices and our beliefs, even as we engage in them.

This first lesson is of a piece with the anti-foundationalism we discussed above. There is no ultimate grounding of any of our beliefs or any of our values. They all arise historically, and are therefore all implicated in the contingencies of that history. There is nowhere we can appeal to as a bedrock of certainty to serve as a standard of evaluation or a basis for building our beliefs. Contingency runs all the way down.

This first lesson should not, however, be taken to lead us to a position of nihilism. This is the second lesson. We cannot infer from the fact of contingency to the conclusion that reflective investigation is futile. Alongside the rejection of foundationalism, and inseparable from it, is holism. The philosopher Wilfrid Sellars sums up holism regarding empirical knowledge this way: "empirical knowledge, like its sophisticated extension, science, is rational, not because it has a *foundation* but because it is a self-correcting enterprise which can put *any* claim in jeopardy, though not *all* at once."[29] This is as precise for our beliefs in values as it is for our beliefs about the empirical world. Philosophy once thought that the threat of nihilism could only be met by the embrace of foundationalism. It is the Cartesian legacy. If there is no bedrock of certainty, if we cannot be sure of any of our beliefs, then we must reject them all. We can no longer hold this position. In abandoning foundationalism, we must also abandon the fear of nihilism with which it is aligned. Such a fear is not only unnecessary; it is incoherent.

The endorsement and rejection of beliefs is a project of reasons. In order to sort out which beliefs we should ratify and which to leave aside, we look for the support those beliefs have. The lesson of anti-foundationalism is that no support is ultimate or absolute. But that does not mean that there is no such thing as support. All of our investigations take place within a historical context in which there are a number of beliefs that are held true and others that are held false. To investigate one of these beliefs as to its acceptability is to ask what reasons support or fail to support it. But those reasons are then held constant; they are, *for the purposes of a particular investigation*, held to be true, or at least unavailable for critique. This is Wittgenstein's lesson that, "Nothing we do can be defended absolutely and finally. But only by reference to something else that is not questioned," and it is the heart of Sellars' claim that while any claim can be placed in jeopardy, we cannot so place all of them at once. Some claims are put in jeopardy in the name of others that are placed, at least momentarily, beyond jeopardy. The rejection of foundationalism teaches us that no claim is immune to jeopardy; holism teaches us that jeopardy is never wholesale.

Foucault's genealogical investigations require a commitment to both anti-foundationalism and holism. He puts certain practices in jeopardy by holding others constant. Among those he holds constant is the integrity of historical investigation. At the outset of his investigation into the history of sexuality, he pauses to pose a question to himself. "Beyond these few phosphorescences, are we not sure to find once more the somber law that always says no [in contrast to his view that power is creative rather than repressive]? The answer will have to come out of a historical inquiry."[30] If the constancy of our sexual character is to be placed in question, it must be on the basis of a historical record that cannot, at least at the moment of investigation, itself be placed in question. Perhaps that record, or the practice of history, can itself come in for genealogical investigation, just as the concepts or terms transhistorically utilized in a particular genealogy can be treated as historical for the purposes of a different genealogy. But that would be another project for another time, and would itself require its own constants.[31]

Our concern here is not with Foucault's *epistemological* constants, but rather with his *normative* ones. Foucault observes that while not everything is bad, everything is dangerous. We know we cannot take this claim to appeal to an ultimate standard for evaluation. There is no foundation for such a normative claim. However, the holism of his anti-foundationalism entails that if some claims are to come in for critique, it is because others are being held constant. If something is dangerous, it is because something else is less dangerous. What holds epistemologically also holds normatively. Both are at once anti-foundationalist and holistic. One can no more critique normatively than one can epistemically without holding something constant.

What are the implicit normative constants in Foucault's work? He suggests none, for reasons we have seen. However, if the argument sketched here is right, he must have one, or some. They are implicit in much of his work. His normativity comes out only periodically and in a suggestive way, such as when he says in the first volume of *The History of Sexuality* that, "The rallying point for the counterattack against the deployment of sexuality ought not to be sex-desire, but bodies and pleasures,"[32] or when he appeals to the term *intolerable* in regard to certain arrangements of power. I would like to suggest that the best way to see Foucault's normative framework is as one that presupposes equality. That is to say, in the face of the Foucauldian question of the grounds of Rancière's embrace of equality, I wish to turn the tables and argue that, given the holism to which Foucault must be committed, it is Rancière's concept of equality that offers a normative framework for the politics of Foucault's genealogies.

We cannot develop this claim in depth here. It would require a more precise treatment of Foucault's texts than is relevant for an understanding of the normative dimension of democratic politics. However, if the suggestion here is right, then two conclusions emerge. First, Rancière's concept of equality can be reconciled with some of strains of recent poststructuralist thought that would seem distant from it. Second, and more important, in the wake of more critical studies, like those of Foucault, we can construct a positive normative conception of political action that does not violate the lessons of such studies, for example the harm of normalization or of speaking for others.

One of the threads that draws Foucault's genealogical works together is the recognition that who we are now is not a product solely of our own making, but also and often more importantly, of practices and interventions of which we are unaware and over which we have little control. More deeply still, the terms in which we conceive ourselves are products of a politically vexed history. We are made to understand who we are, and to be who we are, through a legacy of practices that are at once historically specific and, since we are immersed in that history, unavoidable. The constraints of our history are not necessary. We could have been and we can be otherwise than we are. Nor are they the product of a political conspiracy. Those who benefit from this history are as much its product as those who do not. Though contingent, however, they are the threads of which we are woven; we cannot escape them simply through a decision to do or be otherwise.

If we are to resist the inheritance of this history, we must first understand it. That is the role of the intellectual. Foucault's histories offer a comprehension of the dispersed historical fragments that have intersected, converged, and diverged, in order to make us who we are today. They bring to light the politics of truth in which we find ourselves. "The role of the intellectual is no longer to place himself 'somewhat ahead and to the side' in order to express the stifled truth of the collectivity; rather it is to struggle against the forms of power that transform him into its object and instrument in the sphere of 'knowledge,' 'truth,' 'consciousness,' and 'discourse.' "[33] But understanding is not all. We do not resist or change what we have become merely by recognizing it. We must form new practices, inaugurate new types of truth, experiment with who we might be and who we can be. And we must do this against the grain of a history that has already assigned us our truth and our roles. How are we to accomplish this?

The answer seems clear: through a democratic politics. The constraints Foucault's studies place upon our action are these: we cannot speak in the name of others as to who they are or who they must be; we must be vigilant about the dangers of what we create of ourselves, recognizing that whatever practices we create will have effects of which we are unaware; we must bear in mind that intolerable power relations are not reducible to a single node or center but are dispersed and filtered in our everyday practices. Let us put these constraints in other terms. We must presuppose the equality of each person involved in struggle. We must resist the identities of the police order, but not in the name of another police order. We must not reduce domination to exploitation or any other single form of political or economic relation. Foucault observes that,

> as soon as we struggle against exploitation, the proletariat not only leads the struggle but also defines its targets, its methods, and the places and instruments for confrontation . . . But if the fight is directed against power, then all those on whom power is exercised to their detriment, all who find it intolerable, can begin the struggle on their own terrain and on the basis of their proper activity (or passivity).[34]

If the role of the intellectual is not that of speaking in the name of the collective, and power is dispersed among many practices, each of which is irreducible to – even if intersecting with – other practices, then Foucault's thought, like anarchism, leads to a politics of radical equality. It leads to a politics in which people presuppose themselves equal to those who supervise, monitor, diagnose, teach, categorize, or purport to treat them. It is a politics where people who were the object of intervention become the subject of action, experimenting with who they might be and how they might live. This experimentation is a rejection of the constraints of the existing order – whether those constraints be disciplinary, biopolitical, or otherwise – not in the name of another order with new constraints and new police interventions, but in the name of the equality out of which their experimentation emerges. To experiment in this sense is at once to jettison a particular police order and to refuse to codify one's actions into another one.

Foucault's abandonment of ethics and morality seems largely to stem from a concern that they are forms of dictation of behavior that converge with practices of domination. Moreover, they offer those practices not only a justification but, more deeply, a transcendental grounding. The history of philosophical ethics would seem to provide support for this concern. What makes the normative framework of Rancière's presupposition of equality so compelling is precisely that it rejects this convergence of dictation and domination. It is not that there is no dictation, no constraint, associated with this ethical framework. We have already seen that there is a constraint placed upon the adversaries of a democratic politics – the constraint that emerges from the conflict of a stated embrace of equality with practices that deny it. Moreover, there are constraints placed upon those who act out of the presupposition as well. We have suggested the ideas of trust and sharing as important elements of a democratic politics. Below we will suggest a more traditional ethical obligation, one concerned with violence.

However, what the normative framework of equality accomplishes is to break the link between the constraints of the norms it endorses and the practices of domination fostered by the police order. The reason it accomplishes this has to do with the way the framework situates itself. We saw earlier that while a democratic politics can be justified through an ethics of equality, the ethics of equality in turn arises only in the context of a particular expression of democratic politics. It does not arise from a general philosophical reflection that would seek to ground ethics in a universality divorced from the specifics of the situation in which it is claimed. This does not mean that there is no universal character to the ethics. We have seen that the ethics of equality does have a claim on others. However, this claim, although universal, must arise within the particular situation of a democratic politics; otherwise it becomes a claim placed upon those who are dominated, doubling rather than lifting their domination.

By situating itself within a particular democratic politics, the normative framework we have proposed breaks the link between dictation and domination, the link that is the source of concern about ethics for thinkers like Foucault. If the normative constraints of equality arise only within a democratic politics, then they will not be dedicated to reinforcing the current police order. They will be in the service of its subversion. Unlike the constraints of traditional ethics, the constraints of the ethics of equality do not descend from on high to tell us whom we ought to be or how we ought to act in some overarching way, outside of the specifics of our current situation. That project, the project of a traditional ethics, indeed runs the risk of weaving constraint with domination. Although it does not require the reinforcement of a current police order, the history of philosophy from Mill and Kant to Rawls and Nozick shows that the temptation to draw conclusions in line with such an order is often difficult to resist.

The ethics of a democratic politics does not descend from on high. It emerges from below, from the demands that a democratic politics places through the actions it undertakes and the subjectification it creates. Before there is democratic action, there are no ethical demands. This does not mean that there are no ethical values. Equality remains a value, which is what gives it its justificatory force. However, what equality calls for, the response it claims from those it addresses, can emerge only when there is a democratic politics. Or, more precisely, the claims of equality associated with a democratic politics can emerge only with the appearance of that politics. One may want to claim (and we will return to this in Chapter 5) that the elites have obligations to those who have no part even in the absence of a democratic politics. Otherwise put, there remains an important role for passive equality to play, for now and for the foreseeable future. There can be no question of this. But the demands of equality associated with acting from the presupposition of equality, whether they be upon the elites or upon the actors themselves, do not pre-exist democratic expression. They exist only in situ.

What the normative framework of a democratic politics offers is not a challenge to Foucault's genealogies, or an alternative to it. Nor is it a throwback to a previous period before the lessons of Foucault's thought. It is a precise complement to Foucault's approach. If Foucault offers us the critical awareness of specific police orders, and if he warns us of the dangers of traditional responses to those orders, then a democratic politics – in both its action and its ethical justification – offers a way to conceive action, a way to think about how to move forward in the face of political arrangements it has been Foucault merit to have shown us.

In the French newspaper *Libération*, Rancière writes of Foucault,

> What the materialist history of the conditions of our thought and our action teaches us is neither the necessity of the order of things nor the freedom of subjects. It is the interval between the two, an interval that can only be filled with sentiments such as "the intolerable" that translate no necessity and gesture toward a freedom that is the simple

capacity for action, and not a self-mastery. Between knowledge and action, philosophy founds no deduction. It only creates an interval that opens to us the possibility of making totter the references and certitudes on which various dominations are supported.[35]

Philosophy cannot deduce action from its analyses. We cannot move from Foucault's thought, or that of any other thinker, to a determination of the tasks of politics. Between political analysis and a democratic politics there is, and must be, an interval that only democratic action can fill. What Rancière's thought achieves is to think that interval, not as a deduction but as a possibility. In thinking that interval, the presupposition of equality occupies a central place.

The goal of this chapter has been to show that the embrace of such a presupposition has normative implications. It is not ethically neutral. A democratic politics does not arise without changing the ethical space *in* which it arises. But if this is so, then the challenge is to understand how those changes might occur without returning to a police order and the traditional ethical views with which police orders are aligned. The suggestion we have been following is that the presupposition of equality, because it operates only in action undertaken by those who have no part, can both found an ethics of action and a set of normative constraints entailed by that action. And because of this, such an ethics meets the strictures imposed by a thought like that of Foucault, who lays bare the obstacles faced by any project of contemporary normative thought.

There remain two questions about this ethics, or at least two. The first is interpretive and can be answered quickly: What is the relationship of this ethics to a vision of contemporary anarchism articulated in the last chapter? The second is normative and can only be responded to, at least at this moment, with a theoretical gesture: What, if any, implications for the specifics of political action does this ethical framework have?

The interpretive question concerns the relation of the ethics of Rancière's politics to anarchism. The bond between the two has been gestured at as we have proceeded here. Anarchism's rejection of an avantgarde politics, its concern with the process of political action, its sensitivity to various forms of domination in both society at large and in political communities themselves, and its orientation toward radical equality, are all accounted for in the ethics and politics of the presupposition of equality. What Rancière's work does politically and implies ethically is of a piece with the deepest concerns of much of contemporary anarchism. Moreover, he offers a coherent way to frame those concerns and to bring them forward theoretically. Unlike the tradition of Marxism, anarchism, in its concern for equality, has often been reluctant to engage in theoretical reflection. If what has been said here is correct, that reluctance is unwarranted. There is much to be understood in politics, and many who can contribute to that understanding.

Among what is to be understood, and this is the second remainder, is the question of what, if anything, the ethics of political action implies for the character of political action itself. This is not a question concerning what ought to be done. To approach that question would be to reintroduce the avant-garde, the "indignity of speaking for others." The ethics of political actions asks after the constraints on political action. Does presupposing equality place an ethical burden on those who struggle? Does it require anything of them?

We have already seen two ethical moments: sharing and trust. These, we have noted, are not so much obligations in the traditional sense, as characterizations of the relationships within a democratic politics. In this sense, they contrast with the obligations a democratic politics imposes on those who have a part. For the latter, a democratic politics imposes an ethical burden, an obligation: either act in accordance with the stated principle of equality or recognize that one does not indeed embrace that principle. Does a democratic politics impose internally, among its participants, anything like the obligation it imposes on those it confronts? Are there ethical duties associated with a democratic politics? Does the part that has no part have any ethical obligation toward the part that has a part?

I believe there is such an obligation. It seems to me that the presupposition of equality among those who act cannot remain a presupposition that applies only to those alongside whom one acts. It must also apply to one's adversaries. If those who have no part are to see themselves as equal to those who have a part, then they must also see those who have a part as equal to them. The failure to see one's adversaries as equal to oneself leads not to a destruction of the police order but simply to its inversion. Rather than ending the hierarchies associated with domination, treating those who have a part as less than equal to oneself only reverses the hierarchical roles.

This has implications for political action. There must be an orientation toward – although not an absolute commitment to – nonviolent political action that stems from the presupposition of equality. One must, insofar as possible, refrain from treating those against whom one struggles as beneath consideration, as fair game, or as what Kant would call solely means to one's own ends. This requires political action to be more than just a struggle for suppression of the adversary, even where the adversary engages in cynical domination. It must be creative in its expression of the presupposition of equality.

Nonviolence in politics is often confused with passivity. This is not the place to explain the nature and possibilities of nonviolent action,[36] however it must be understood that nonviolence often lies at the opposite pole from political passivity, further away from it than violent resistance. Violent resistance remains in many cases the norm. One is dominated, so one dominates; one is oppressed, so one oppresses. In that sense, violence is always the easy political option. It reverses the power in a relationship. Violence is the natural temptation for those raised in a police order. It requires only that those who have no part imagine themselves in the place of those who do, and imagine those who do taking their place.

What nonviolence can achieve is something else: not a reversal of power but an effacing of the terms in which a context of power has been conceived. In the framework of a political orientation whose task is to declassify, nonviolent action carries with it more radical possibilities for declassification than the simple inversion that is the standard consequence of violent resistance. This is because nonviolence must reject the type of thinking fostered by a police order. It requires the creation of a non-hierarchical space, a space where the expression of a political subject is not defined by its striving for a place in the social hierarchy but instead by a self-creation unencumbered by a concern for its place vis-à-vis the other.

In this sense, although not in many others, nonviolent action touches upon a Nietzschean theme. For Nietzsche, the distinction between active and reactive forces is that the latter define themselves in relation to the former while the former define themselves by their own creative activity. Reactive forces are driven by resentment; they *react* to their world in fear and loathing rather than creating something that contributes to or alters that world. Active forces are unconcerned with reactive forces. They create, and in the course of creating sometimes destroy, without concern for their own relation to other forces, whether active or reactive. They are defined by what they do rather than by what they oppose.[37] While it might be tempting to associate democratic politics with reactive forces, since they oppose a current police order rather than seeking to create a new one, this would be to neglect an essential point. Democratic politics is defined not by opposition, but by its declassifying presupposition of equality.

It is democratic politics, then, which is creative and oriented toward change. It is not wedded to the terms in which it arises, and does not need the security of new (police) terms. Moreover, it is not oriented in relation to what it opposes, by an inequality relative to others that must be maintained, but first and foremost by its own presupposition that motivates action.

This analogy should not be carried too far. It indicates the difference between action as a creation and action as a reaction. However, for Nietzsche, active forces are entirely unconcerned with other forces. Whether those forces are destroyed in the course of an active creation has no bearing. Here Nietzsche's path diverges from that of nonviolence. Nonviolence is creative activity within the constraints provided by recognizing the equality of others. When African American students sat down at the lunch counter in Greensboro, when Gandhi led the Salt March in protest at British salt taxes, when gays perform commitment ceremonies, when librarians refuse to turn over the borrowing histories of their patrons to federal snoopers, they are envisioning other forms of social relationships, forms that do not express one's own equality at the expense of the equality of others but instead alongside it.

Nonviolent political action is the most direct expression of a democratic politics that seeks to express equality without denying the equality of others. Does this mean that violent struggle is never justified? Of course not. There are certainly times when self-protection requires that one act with violence against one's adversaries. I believe, although will not defend that belief here, that those times are far fewer than many people imagine, even in the face of violence. However, it would be a stringent requirement on political action to reject violent struggle at the outset. The more urgent question facing a democratic politics is not that of whether violence is ever justified, but whether it can be reconciled with a democratic politics. Can a struggle be both violent and democratic?

The question here is not the traditional one of whether a violent resistance struggle tends to become internally undemocratic. History has largely answered that question in the affirmative, although one might still argue that history does not need to have the last word here. Our question lies elsewhere. If one of the ethical constraints on a democratic politics is that of recognizing the equality of one's adversaries, is it possible to commit violence against that adversary without betraying that recognition? It seems that violent struggle requires one to choose between one's own worthiness and that of one's adversary.

If this is so, then would it not follow that violence necessarily involves a decision in favor of inequality? I must decide who is to be harmed or killed; that decision cannot be made within the confines of universal equality, the normative framework of a democratic politics. Somebody is to be made less than equal.

One can imagine the precise point at which the decision about violence would arise. In the discussion of the ethics of a democratic politics with regard to the adversary, we saw that acting on the presupposition of equality places those who have a part in an either/or position. Either they can embrace equality and endorse the politics with which they are faced, or they can admit that they do not really believe in equality. Because ethics, like the rest of philosophy, has no conceptual foundations that force a decision either way, both paths are open. In a nominally democratic society, it is unlikely that one would choose the second option (although, of course, there are ways of seeking to maintain inequality while pretending to oneself that one still favors equality). However, it is still possible to do so. And in a society in which equality does not even receive lip service, there is less that bars that option.

If the part that has a part simply denies the equality of those engaged in democratic struggle, then the stage is set for violence. A democratic politics that has forced a decision on equality and is faced with its denial seems to have little choice but to force the issue against those who deny it. This does not mean that violence is a necessary option. In the civil rights movement, for instance, the denial of equality persisted in much of the white South for years in the face of nonviolent struggle before it was – at least for the purposes of legislation – finally worn down. In an alternative case, during the first *intifada* in 1988, while Israel never recognized the equality of the Palestinians, it was forced to act differently toward them by the pressure of world opinion. However, if the adversaries of a democratic politics persist in denying the equality of those who have no part, it is possible that the time will come when nonviolent struggle cannot, at least by itself, create the conditions under which equality can flourish. The question then arises of whether the violent continuation of struggle is still a democratic politics, or whether it is a return to a traditional politics of inequality.

This question underscores a point we raised earlier about the conditions for most democratic politics. Although a democratic politics is a dissensus from a police order, in most cases this dissensus is not a complete one. Democratic politics does not usually reject the entirety of a particular police order, a particular partition and distribution of the sensible. There is a point of consensus that can bind a politics of equality to the police order it rejects: an agreement on the equality of everyone in the order itself. It is precisely this agreement that allows democratic struggle to gain a nonviolent foothold on the police order. While this point of consensus may be obscured in the struggle, it often exists; and nonviolent struggle is the most likely path to find it.

We should not make too much of this point of consensus. It generally does not form a ground from which normative discussion of the kind Jürgen Habermas promotes would be able to arise. For Habermas, the recognition of consensus is the starting point for normative discussion. For a democratic politics, by contrast, while the endorsement of equality may be contained in a given police order (an endorsement that is in conflict with much of the practices of that order), the *recognition* of that equality by those who have a part lies at the end rather than at the beginning of a democratic politics.

However, what if that recognition is not forthcoming, and the turn to violence is made? Do we still have a democratic politics? I am tempted to say that a democratic politics can remain, although one is at its outer edge. There seems no bar to placing side by side the claims that one's adversary is one's equal and that, because of the adversary's refusal to recognize one's own equality, one must injure or kill her. The analogy here would be one of self-defense. To defend oneself against another does not require a denial of that other's equality. It requires instead an embrace of one's own. Self-protection is, or at least can be, defined in terms not of a specific attitude toward the other, but of the necessity of preserving oneself. So it is with a violent democratic struggle. The emergence of violence in such a struggle arises on the basis of a persistence in one's own equality, of the effort to maintain the expression of the presupposition of equality in the face of steadfast refusal to allow that expression. Seen in these terms, although the effect of violence may be a denial of the other, it is not because of the attempt to deny the other but to preserve one's own democratic expression that violence can be resorted to without violating the ethical strictures of a democratic politics.

If this is right, then one can see that the appeal to violence in the context of democratic struggle lies on a razor's edge. The line between self-preservation and the denial of the equality of the other is a thin one. Moreover, violence tempts one to step over that line. Caught up in the moment of violence, it is easy to ratify the destruction of the other out of anger for the denial one has suffered rather than for the preservation of one's democratic expression. The deeper the history of denial of equality, the stronger that temptation is. In this sense, the normative framework of democratic politics provides a corrective. By placing the emphasis of violent struggle on self-preservation rather than destruction of the other, it can help mitigate some of the more deleterious aspects of violent struggle. This provides no guarantee of safeguards against abuse. However, it does point toward a more adequate conception of the role of violence in political struggle than is characteristic of the practice of violence in many of the struggles that have unfolded in the name of democracy.

Notes

1. For one example of this assumption at work, see Judith D. Hoover and Leigh Anne Howard's "The Political Correctness Controversy Revisited: Retreat from Argumentation and Reaffirmation of Critical Dialogue," in *American Behavioral Scientist*, Vol. 38, No. 7, June/July 1995, pp. 963–75.
2. Gilles Deleuze and Michel Foucault, "Intellectuals and Power," in Michel Foucault, *Language, Counter-Memory, Practice: Selected Essays and Interviews*. ed. Donald F. Bouchard, tr. Donald F. Bouchard and Sherry Simon. Ithaca, NY: Cornell University Press, 1977 (or. pub. 1972), p. 209.
3. Martin Rue, "Truth, Power, Self: An Interview with Michel Foucault," in Luther H. Martin, Huck Gutman, and Patrick Hutton (eds), *Technologies of the Self*. Amherst, MA: University of Massachusetts Press, 1988 (interview conducted in 1982), p. 11.
4. Gilles Deleuze, *Spinoza: Practical Philosophy*. tr. Robert Hurley. San Francisco: City Light Books, 1988 (or. pub. 1970), p. 23.
5. Ludwig Wittgenstein, *Culture and Value*, ed. G. H. von Wright, tr. Peter Winch. Chicago: University of Chicago Press, 1980, p. 16. I discuss this idea and the metaethics in which it is embedded at more length in *The Moral Theory of Poststructuralism*, University Park, PA: Penn State Press, 1995, Chapter 1.
6. On the idea of implicit commitments following conscious ones, and of making implicit commitments explicit, see Robert Brandom's *Making it Explicit* (Cambridge, MA: Harvard University Press, 1994).
7. Cited in Rancière, "The Uses of Democracy," p. 46.
8. I discuss this at more length in the first chapter of *The Moral Theory of Poststructuralism*.
9. Rancière, "The Community of Equals," in *On the Shores of Politics*, p. 86.
10. Rancière, "Ten Theses on Politics," p. 10.

11. Rancière, *Disagreement*, p. 58.
12. Rancière, "Ten Theses on Politics," pp. 6–7.
13. Rancière, *Disagreement*, p. 139.
14. Rancière, "The Uses of Democracy," p. 49.
15. Rancière, "The Uses of Democracy," p. 61.
16. For the original French, see *Aux bords du politique* (Paris: Gallimard, 1998), pp. 94 and 111. The last phrase of the second passage, which the translator has rendered "founded on trust," is *c'est-à-dire confiant*. This is more literally rendered as "that is to say, trusting." The more literal rendering does not put trust beneath democracy's self-image but within it.
17. Immanuel Kant, *Groundwork of the Metaphysic of Morals*, p. 101.
18. Carol Gilligan, *In a Different Voice: Psychological Theory and Women's* pp. 16–17.
19. David Hume, *A Treatise of Human Nature*. Second Edition. Oxford: Clarendon Press, 1978 (or. pub. 1739), p. 316.
20. Rancière, *Disagreement*, p. 39.
21. Another difference between Foucault and Kuhn is that while Foucault treats what are termed the "human sciences," Kuhn is concerned with the "hard sciences" such as physics and chemistry. Joseph Rouse argues that the latter are just as vulnerable to Foucaultian critique as the former. Cf. *Knowledge and Power: Toward a Political Philosophy of Science* (Ithaca, NY: Cornell University Press, 1990), and *Engaging Science: How to Understand its Practices Philosophically* (Ithaca, NY: Cornell University Press, 1996).
22. Michel Foucault, *The History of Sexuality, Vol. 1: An Introduction*, tr. Robert Hurley. New York: Random House, 1978 (or. pub. 1976), p. 94.
23. Foucault, *History of Sexuality*, p. 94.
24. Foucault, *History of Sexuality*, p. 12.
25. Foucault, *History of Sexuality*, p. 69.
26. Foucault, *History of Sexuality*, p. 78.
27. Michel Foucault, "The Ethic of Care for the Self as a Practice of Freedom" (an interview), in James Bernauer and David Rasmussen, *The Final Foucault*. Cambridge, MA: MIT Press, 1988, p. 18.
28. Michel Foucault, "Politics and Ethics: An Interview," tr. Catherine Porter, in Paul Rabinow, *The Foucault Reader*. New York: Pantheon, 1984, p. 343.
29. Wilfrid Sellars, "Empiricism and the Philosophy of Mind," in *Science, Perception, and Reality*. London: Routledge & Kegan Paul, 1963, p. 170.
30. Foucault, *History of Sexuality, Vol. 1*, p. 72.
31. I investigate Foucault's anti-foundationalism and holism at greater length in *Between Genealogy and Epistemology: Psychology, Politics, and Knowledge in the Thought of Michel Foucault*. University Park, PA: Penn State Press, 1993, esp. Chapters 5 and 6.

32. Foucault, *History of Sexuality, Vol. 1*, p. 157.

33. Foucault, "Intellectuals and Power," p. 208.

34. Foucault, "Intellectuals and Power," p. 216. Note that at this point Foucault has not entirely developed the nuanced view of power that characterizes his mature genealogical work, and so it seems that power itself, rather that certain of its appearances, is to be resisted.

35. Jacques Rancière, "Les philosophes san porte-voix," *Libération*, June 25, 2004. www.liberation.fr/imprimer.php?Article=216733.

36. The classic statement of the nature and possibilities of nonviolent action remains Gene Sharp's three-volume *The Politics of Nonviolent Action*. The first volume, *Power and Struggle* (Boston: Porter Sargent, 1973) explains the dynamic of nonviolence: its general orientation and unfolding. It shows how different nonviolent is from political passivity.

37. Cf. Friedrich Nietzsche, *On the Genealogy of Morals*. tr. Douglass Smith. Oxford: Oxford University Press, 1996 (or. pub. 1887), esp. the second essay. For an interpretation of the relation of active and reactive forces, see Gilles Deleuze's *Nietzsche and Philosophy*. tr. Hugh Tomlinson. New York: Columbia University Press, 1983 (or. pub. 1962), Chapter 2.

CHAPTER 5

Active Equality in Contemporary Politics

The discourse of democratic politics is addressed to people who are politically dispossessed, that is to say, us. Not to all of us, perhaps. There may be those who read these words that have no need of or interest in a democratic politics, those for whom inequalities tilt largely in their favor. And, of course, at the other end of things, there will be many who do not have access to books like these. They have been deprived of the means – the money, the education, the time – to grapple with the reflections we are considering here. Although spoken to, they will be, in this medium at least, unable to be spoken with.

Nevertheless, the framework of active equality that Rancière has placed before us is theoretically revolutionary, in the way that Thomas Paine's *Common Sense* is revolutionary. It is a framework that does not speak to the elites of their obligations, but to the demos of their possibilities. It is not a discourse of duty, nor is it a discourse of rights. It is a discourse of emancipation. Unlike mainstream political theory, Rancière's articulation of active equality is not commissioned by a tradition whose discussants are those who have a part.[1] It does not tell them what they owe to the people or what they deserve from them. The theory of democratic politics turns its back on those who benefit from the inequalities of the police order. They will reappear later, as respondents rather than participants.

Addressed to the many of us who, in different and various ways, suffer the burden of inequality, democratic politics offers us, not a way to be liberated, but a way to think about how to liberate ourselves. It can assist us in moving from the gated communities of our lives toward a future that is at once common and nonconformist. Democratic politics "is a matter of interpreting, in the theatrical sense of the word, the gap between the place where the demos exists and a place where it does not, where there are only populations, individuals, employers and employees, heads of households and spouses, and so on."[2] Democratic politics creates a people where there was none before, turning workers into the proletariat, Palestinians into the Palestinian people, women into the feminist movement.

On the ground of a people, a community arises. "Democracy is the community of sharing, in both senses of the term: a membership in a single world which can only be expressed in adversarial terms, and a coming together which can only occur in conflict."[3] When people come together in sharing and trust and in an expression of equality against the police order, they form a community. Not a community of the subjected, in Foucault's sense of the term, but a community of subjectification in the active sense, the sense in which those who have taken hold of their lives ensure that they are subjects rather than objects. Whether this can only occur in conflict is an issue we will return to below. That, in our world, it can only occur in conflict cannot be denied. The police orders that are the ether of our lives preclude any other possibility.

That ether often appears natural or inevitable. As I remarked at the outset, we have become politically passive. Through hopelessness, complacency, fear (a fear that, as I write, is the incessant drumbeat of the current U.S. administration), we assume our allotted places, obediently if not happily. We shoulder the role of workers and, if we are fortunate, of consumers. We remain isolated from one another, caught in a web that, while it cannot be escaped without our intervention, is not of our making. It is a web, moreover, that presents itself as inescapable. Things could not be different from the way they are now. If there ever was such a thing as solidarity, that happened in another place, another time. You are alone, the police order tells us. We can assist you, but only on the condition that you remain alone. Solidarity is dangerous and probably subversive. In the wake of the events of September 11, 2001, Americans received a single message from their president. It was not to form communities or organizations. It was not to sacrifice themselves for others. It was not even to recognize that others exist. It was, to shop.

So we shop. And our purchases, while they make our lives less burdensome, do not lend them meaning or significance. After the initial thrill of the purchase, we are left strangely bereft, like an addict after the rush of her drug.[4] We do not know what else to do, so, as an addict would, we return to the scene of our transient pleasure. Or we retreat to the privacy of our home, shoring it up against an external world that for reasons both obvious and elusive appears increasingly threatening. Or we lose ourselves in work, finding reasons to stay there longer than necessary, creating our own erotics of the workplace:

feeling the soft padding of the carpet under our feet when we can remove our shoes, discovering a womb in the silence after hours.

It is precisely here that the voice of a democratic politics can speak to us: where we are most imprisoned in our passivity. What a democratic politics offers us is the one thing the police order forbids, the single most threatening possibility facing the continuation of any order of inequality: hope. It is a hope that is not given to us. No theory, not Rancière's or any other can do that. Any theory that claims to give us hope has already taken it away. Rather, it is a hope that remains for us to create. What the voice of democratic politics tells us is not *Here is your hope*. It is that *We are not barred from hope*. It is not there before us, in a place that already exists, awaiting our grasp. This is not because it cannot exist. It does not exist, but it can be made. It can be made, though, only if we choose to make it. Only if we create ourselves as the subjects of our lives, struggling alongside others against the police order that forbids us hope. Even then, we will not find our hope at the end of our struggle. Our hope is in the struggle itself, in the expression of equality that it is and in the community that forms around it.

It is at this point where the discourse of democratic politics diverges most sharply from that of traditional political theory. Because it addresses us, Rancière's politics offers us hope instead of, or better alongside, our duties. Distributive theories of justice, because they concern themselves with what is owed to people, can offer people nothing more than the obligations of others. Whether those obligations are material, social, or, as with Nozick, simply obligations of non-interference, they come to us rather than from us. They may allow us the space to create our lives, and thus access to some hope for the future, but when they do they are, at best, one step away from hope. And even then, because we are passive, the hope they offer can never entirely be ours. It depends on others at least as much as it depends on us. In a democratic politics, since the moment of active equality is at the same time and in the same gesture the moment of self-creation, hope is folded into political expression. It is a politics of hope, rather than a politics that offers the resources out of which a person may, if she overcomes her role as recipient, create a bit of hope.

Passivity, even when it is passive equality, is a thin reed upon which to balance the prospect of hope.

None of this is to suggest that hope, or the politics that creates it, is an easy task. Politics happens rarely, Rancière reminds us. The police orders to which we are subject do not brook resistance gladly.

Moreover, the political passivity our world impresses upon us is a difficult legacy to overcome. It is reinforced not only by our theories but also by the institutions and practices through which and by which we live. Indeed, our theories may be the least of these. The current collusion between the power of states and the dominance of the market, reinforced by the fear of terrorism, converges on an exclusion of any specifically *political* hope. Hope, we are told, is economic, not political; private, not public.

The question that remains before us, then, is how we might begin to think democratic politics in our current world? If, until now, we have remained at the level of theory, considering the nature of democratic politics, we must turn finally to ask how this theory intervenes upon the state of things. Where are equality and its hope in the world we inhabit now? What are their prospects?

It cannot be a question here of a political program. To offer such a program would betray what we have insisted upon throughout – that democratic politics emerges from the demos. Instead, we must remain content to point to ways in which democratic politics is being denied in our world as well as to openings the world offers to it. For the rest, it is the task of action. If anarchism, in its history, has been too reliant on action at the expense of theoretical reflection, its insistence that nothing changes solely by means of theory is undeniable. Democratic politics is not a spectator sport. We do not watch the theorist in reflection and become emancipated. Nevertheless, in leaving our reflections at the doorstep of action, we can point out strategies that serve to blunt the force of active equality and places where openings lie before us.

In approaching this task, we will proceed in three stages. First, we will follow Rancière's own discussion of the European context. In several recent works, he has offered an analysis of the ways in which European politics has acted to diffuse and marginalize the possibility of democratic politics. This will open out onto a more general discussion of globalization, the obstacles to active equality it creates and the opportunities we might find in it. Finally, we will turn to the question of whether a democratic politics can be institutionalized. Rancière claims that the politics of active equality cannot be institutionalized, which denies all permanency to democratic expression. I would like to question this conclusion, on the basis of some of Rancière's own concepts. I will do so, not in favor of the idea that a democratic politics *can* be institutionalized, but that perhaps it *might* be. The move is not from atheism to belief, but from atheism to agnosticism. It is a small shift, but the

political stakes are high. They require a change from despair about permanency to a call for experimentations with its possibility.

In his writings of the 1990s, Rancière refers to the European political context as one of *consensus*. More recently, while not abandoning the term, he introduces the term *ethics* to describe a changed
context. While the latter context is more continuous with U.S. politics, the former is more specifically European. It derives from the particular role that bureaucracy plays in European political life, and
specifically in relation to economics. As a first gesture toward understanding, we can recall that while the U.S. has a single national government, Europe is governed in a multitude of states, but is at the
same time experimenting with unity through the European Union.

What, then, is consensus? Rancière writes that consensus democracy, or what he sometimes calls *post-democracy*, is

> the paradox that, in the name of democracy, emphasizes the consen-
> sual practice of effacing the forms of democratic action. Postdemocracy
> is the government practice and conceptual legitimization of a democ-
> racy *after* the demos, a democracy that has eliminated the appearance,
> miscount, and dispute of the people and is thereby reducible to the sole
> interplay of state mechanisms and combinations of social energies and
> interests . . . This is the actual meaning of what is called consensus
> democracy.[5]

Consensus is a contemporary attempt to end politics, to move beyond
the struggle it involves. It envisions a seamless world with no room for
disagreement or dissensus. The consensus toward which the European
politics of the 1990s aims substitutes management for politics.

Consensus centers itself on technological solutions to political
problems. To grasp this, it is perhaps worth using French politics as
an example. In France, those who eventually occupy positions of official political leadership emerge from a small number of select schools,
such as the *Écoles Normales Supérieures* or the *École Polytechnique*.
At the administrative branches of these schools, one learns, in essence,
how to run a state. The running of a state is a technological problem,
and what the student receives is both technological know-how and,
more important, the belief that that know-how is the central aspect
of politics. (It is perhaps no surprise, for instance, that the *École
Polytechnique*, which has contributed a number of French political
leaders, specializes in engineering.) Students graduate with a body of
technical knowledge, a commitment to public service, a set of beliefs
about what public service involves, and a group of peers that she will

spend her professional years among. These peers share the knowledge, commitment, and beliefs of one another. "Postdemocracy is perhaps the precise coincidence of ochlocracy with its supposed opposite, *epistemocracy*: government by the most intelligent, emerging quite naturally from the regime of the education system to effect the precisely calculated administration of the infinity of great and small focuses of satisfaction."[6]

This system converges with two determining aspects of the European context. The first is neoliberalism. Although there has been much made of the distinction between the U.S. commitment to neoliberalism and France's resistance to it, France is not immune to the neoliberal context in which all states are forced currently to operate. What distinguishes the French, and more broadly European, approach to neoliberalism from that of the U.S. is that it is tempered by a concern for those are not neoliberalism's direct beneficiaries. While in the U.S. the paring away of state services (except those associated with the military) leaves people to their own devices, Europe is more oriented toward a social safety net. Nevertheless, common to both is the view that the political sphere is subservient to the economic one. Otherwise put, capitalist economic development is the answer to questions that once may have seemed political, and the role of the state is to help create the conditions for the efficient (and, in Europe, minimally humane) functioning of a capitalist market.[7] Rancière sums up this move (substituting the term *social* for my term *economic*) in the following passage:

> This primary task of politics can be indeed precisely described in modern terms as the political reduction of the social (that is to say the distribution of wealth) and the social reduction of the political (that is to say the distribution of various powers and the imaginary investments attached to them). On the one hand, to quiet the conflict of rich and poor through the distribution of rights, responsibilities, and controls; on the other, to quiet the passions aroused by the occupation of the centre by virtue of spontaneous social activities.[8]

To ensure that inequality is veiled, everyone is accorded a particular place in the political order, and to ensure that political division is veiled, everyone is accorded a place (or at least a minimum standard of living) in the economic order. On the one hand, there are the political technocrats from the elite schools who are at the top, and those who carry out – or, for most people, become the recipients of – the technological solutions they propose in descending order below them.

On the other hand, there are the solutions themselves, designed to blunt the force of dissensus by giving everyone a stake in the status quo. Those who refuse are not resisters, they are simply people who have not yet understood the benevolence of the order. They are atavistic, like the racists who oppose the free mobility of labor through their vicious attacks on immigrants. "[F]or all the troubles of consensus, the oligarchs, their savants and their ideologues, have found the explanation: if science has not imposed its legitimacy, it is because of ignorance. If progress does not progress, it is because of those who remain backwards [*retardataires*]."[9]

This technological approach to neoliberalism converges with other aspects of the European context: integration and the European Union. The emergence of transnational political entities such as the European Commission and the Council of European Union distance the people from their political "representatives" even further than they are in their national states. Without input from the *demos*, European legislators seek to determine the economic policies of their constituting states.[10] Again, we should emphasize that this determination is often far more humane than the national policies characteristic of the United States, particularly in areas like wages, unemployment compensation, and day care. However, what is of moment here is that the intersection of neoliberalism and European integration points the way toward a technological interpretation of and approach to political issues.

This technological approach amounts to a project of de-politicization. In the name of discussion and consensus, political leadership seeks to reduce struggles around equality to technical issues of economic progress and distribution. There is no division between those who have a part and those who do not. If there are inequalities, this is either because some inequality is needed in order to maintain economic progress, or because that progress has not yet fully blossomed. What there cannot be, in the technological approach, is dissensus. We are all agreed, all living in a single world, in seamless agreement about what should be done. "The consensus system announced a world beyond the demos, a world made up of individuals and groups simply showing common humanity. It overlooked just one thing: between individuals and humanity, there is always a participation of the sensible: a configuration that determines the way in which the parties have a part in the community."[11] In short, what the consensus system neglects is that equality granted is not really equality. Equality is not given, it is taken – or better, presupposed and expressed.

The technological approach to politics is not far from the traditional liberal political philosophy we considered in the first chapter. It is concerned with the distribution of goods rather than with the participation of people in the creation of their lives. What distinguishes European consensus from liberal theory is its focus on capitalist economics. Although Rawls' and Sen's respective approach to justice may be captured within a capitalist economic system, broadly defined (certainly not an unfettered free market, as would be the case for Nozick), there is nothing in their theories that requires a capitalist system. Whether or not capitalism, or, say, some form of market socialism would be the economic system most likely to realize their distributive principles is a purely empirical matter, and thus does not concern them at the level of theory. By contrast, European politics begins from a capitalist context, which it takes for granted, since it is our context. This difference aside, the convergence on what we have called passive equality is unmistakable in both.

Near the end of his 1995 book *Disagreement* (*La Mésentente*), Rancière refers to a second movement, one that stands alongside and is entwined with consensus to co-determine Europe's political, or better apolitical, context. He calls this second movement *ethics*. His description of it is, at this point, philosophically based. Ethics is "the proposition put to philosophy to eliminate itself, to leave it to the absolute Other to atone for the flaws in the notion of the Same."[12] For those who are philosophically minded, the reference to the thought of Emmanuel Levinas is unmistakable.

In Levinas' view, ethics cannot be based on a set of ethical principles. The problem with principles is that they reduce the other to my own categories. If I act toward the other based upon principles I carry with me previous to and outside of my interaction with the other, then it is not really the other I am concerned with. I am imposing my ethical framework upon the other, rather than taking up the other in her own right. What must substitute for ethical principles, then, is an obligation to the other *as* other, as different from and irreducible to any of my own principles. In his book *Totality and Infinity*, Levinas refers to this type of obligation as that of infinity, contrasting it with the totality (with its resonance with totalitarianism) characteristic of traditional philosophical thought. "It is a relationship with *a surplus always exterior to the totality*, as though the objective totality did not fill out the true measure of being, as though another concept, the concept of *infinity*, were needed to express this transcendence with regard to totality, non-encompassable within a totality and as primordial as totality."[13]

The term *infinity* captures the direction of Levinas' thought aptly. Infinity cannot be conceived. Whatever limit we want to impose upon it conceptually, it always extends beyond that limit. Although it can be gestured at in thought, it cannot be grasped by the thought that gestures toward it. "Infinity is characteristic of a transcendent being as transcendent; the infinite is the absolutely other."[14] Although there is a place where infinity expresses itself – the face of the other – that place does not offer itself for capture. The face of the other is where I become obliged to that which transcends my ability to understand. It is that vulnerability to which I am called to be vulnerable myself.

What is the proper ethical relation to the infinitely other? It is one of infinite obligation. The other, the face of the other, calls me in her otherness, obliges me without respite. "The 'You shall not commit murder' which delineates the face in which the Other is produced submits my freedom to judgment."[15] I am never done with my obligation to the other. It always lies before me, and in that sense my life is never wholly my own. It is infused with obligations that I can neither refuse nor finally satisfy.

The political problem with such an ethics is that it abandons the possibility of democratic solidarity.[16] The relation between self and other in Levinas' approach is grounded on a double asymmetry rather than equality. Instead of a community of equals, there is an inequality running from other to self and back from self to other. The face of the other reveals a vulnerability to which I am called to respond. That vulnerability is the first asymmetry. My being called is the second one. The first asymmetry concerns the fact that the face of the other presents itself as exposed to me, naked and defenseless. A face cannot be defended from attack. On the other hand, that very exposure is what calls me, what obliges me in its very defenselessness. I never cease being obliged to the other, ethically prostate before her. To commit violence upon her is not to deny an obligation; it is to refuse to recognize an obligation that is always already there. In this double asymmetry, there is never a *we*. The *you* and the *I* in our double asymmetry are never surmounted into a community of equals.

Those who would defend Levinas here may point out, correctly, that the *you* and the *I* are not entirely divorced. My obligation to you (and yours to me) does not exist outside of who I am. I am partially constituted by my obligation to you in your otherness. That is why I am never entirely present to myself. Who I am is not self-contained, but is also composed of an obligation that transcends my ability to conceive it. Otherwise put, I am never entirely present to myself, since who I am is in part an experience of obligation to an infinitely other. This is why, for Levinas, ethics, or what he sometimes calls *metaphysics*, must precede ontology. "Metaphysics, transcendence, the welcoming of the other by the same, of the Other by me, is concretely produced as the calling into question of the same by the other, that is, as the ethics that accomplishes the critical essence of knowledge. And as critique precedes dogmatism, metaphysics precedes ontology."[17] Or, more trenchantly, "Morality is not a branch of philosophy, but first philosophy."[18]

That my obligation to the other is partially constitutive of who I am can be granted as part of Levinas' view. This changes nothing, however, with regard to the formation of a collective political subject. The interiorization of the double asymmetry, the bringing of it into myself, no more yields equality than it would if it were exterior to me. As long as ethics is a matter of vulnerability rather than equality, it remains beholden to an ethics of inequality, or, more precisely, an ethics of mutual inequality. In Levinas' view, I am at once above and below the other: capable of violence toward her (even if that violence is only that of denying her otherness, of reducing her to my own categories) and obliged to her out of that capability. We do not occupy the same level. In politics, we must seek each other on a common ethical ground, one that supports both of us rather than allowing each to slide beneath the other. This common ethical ground, as we saw in Chapter 2, does not require that we all be alike, that the other be reduced to my own categories. It requires only that we commit ourselves to our own equality with the other. In an ethics that is to serve as a framework for politics, there can be neither masters nor slaves, even where the slaves are also masters and the masters also slaves.

This does not mean that there cannot be vulnerability in democratic political expression. We saw in Chapter 4 that both sharing and trust have a vulnerable, indeed asymmetrical, character. However, sharing and trust arise *within* a political relationship of presupposed equality. It is only because I am acting on the presupposition of our mutual equality that I can engage in sharing and trust. Equality is founding for vulnerability rather than, as in Levinas, the other way around.

For Rancière, the contemporary political expression of Levinas' ethical approach lies in the humanitarian justifications for intervention given in the 1990s in places like Bosnia and Somalia. He does not deny, of course, that there were humanitarian crises in these countries. Rather, he sees humanitarianism as a new form of the blunting of politics. What humanitarianism accomplishes is to place people in the position of victim. Instead of acting in solidarity with those who struggle, humanitarianism places those who might struggle in the position of recipients of aid or intervention. They are to be helped because they cannot help themselves. As with Levinas' view, it is the vulnerability of the victims that obliges us rather than their equality to us.

What this leads to, politically, is humanitarian intervention rather than solidarity. We are called to assist the victim in her vulnerability rather than to stand alongside them in struggle. It is not the equality of the other, but precisely the opposite – her inequality – that moves me. Think here of the advertisements appealing for aid for deprived peoples. They invariably display the face, often of a child, in its vulnerability or powerlessness. The message this conveys is straightforward: these people are helpless; you are not; you must reach down and help them.

Humanitarian assistance is, while certainly necessary at moments, profoundly apolitical. It is a counter-movement to democratic politics. And to the degree to which it substitutes itself for such a politics, the ability to act in solidarity under the banner of equality is compromised.

Rancière sees a collusion between this kind of humanitarianism and Europe's technological approach to politics.

> Political action finds itself today trapped in a pincer movement between state managerial police and the world police of humanitarianism. On the one hand, the logics of consensus systems efface the traces of political appearance, miscount, and dispute. On the other, they summon politics, driven from the scene, to set itself up from the position of a globalization of the human that is a globalization of the victim, a definition of the sense of the world and of a community of humanity based on the figure of the victim.[19]

The dynamic of this convergence is not difficult to see. On one side, people are told that any dissensus is retrograde; it is a sign that one does not yet understand the working of the global economic system and the role that politics is supposed to play in it. Politics is a matter of coming to agreement on the proper conditions for and parameters of a global market economy. On the other side, those who suffer, for whatever reason, are victims. This leaves two options, one for peoples and the other for states.

The option for peoples is humanitarian assistance: charity, rather than solidarity. The option for states is intervention. On behalf of those who suffer, be they Kosovans, Sudanese, or Iraqis, the states of the West can intervene in their name into conflicts or states that victimize them. In any case, the intervention of states is not *with* or *alongside* peoples (as anarchists have long recognized, states cannot do this), but *for* them. Neither option involves a democratic politics. The figure of the victim precludes it. "The rights of man were once the weapon of dissidents, opposing another people to those the State pretended to incarnate. They have become the rights of populations victimized by the new ethnic wars, the rights of individuals chased from their destroyed homes, of violated women or massacred men."[20]

The figure of the victim has become more prominent in Rancière's recent political writings. Particularly since September 11, 2001, the politics of the victim has begun to occupy center-stage in the strategy of eliminating democratic expression. In discussing its emergence, Rancière focuses less on its theoretical grounding in a Levinasian ethics, and more on a politics of pure evil. The most prominent theoretical touchstone here is perhaps Jean-François Lyotard's invocation of the Kantian concept of the sublime.[21] However, a more perspicuous approach is through the recent European appropriation of the Holocaust.

In the early postwar period, the interpretation of the Holocaust was dominated by "the determination of the Western democracies in the struggle against a totalitarianism always in place or at least threatening."[22] The Holocaust was a product of Nazism, which was in turn a matter of totalitarianism, and in that sense, its affinities lay with communism and with all political movements that reject Western democracy. During the 1970s and 1980s, though, another interpretation of the Holocaust emerged.

> It made of these crimes [against the Jews] not only the monstrous effects of a regime that was to be struggled against, but the forms of manifestation of an infinite crime, unthinkable and irreparable, the work of a power of Evil exceeding all juridical and political measure. Ethics has become the thought of this evil, creating a irremediable break in history.[23]

This new interpretation, which we might associate not only with Lyotard but also with Theodor Adorno, Jacques Derrida, Jean-Luc Nancy, and Philippe Lacoue-Labarthe,[24] takes the Holocaust to be not merely an egregious crime committed under certain historical conditions, but a revelation of something much deeper, of what Rancière calls evil. This evil is more ontological than historical in character, although the Holocaust, as a historical event, creates an "irremediable break" with the past in revealing this evil to us, in giving the lie to any myth of human progress. (To be precise: for thinkers who write in the Heideggerian tradition, the problem lies in the entire trajectory of the Western tradition, in its appropriation of Being, rather than in Being itself or the being of humans.) Evil is not amenable to specific historical analyses or political overcoming. At best, it can be kept at bay through continuous political intervention, through a project of what President George Bush called (before the Christian right took him to task for invoking God's powers) *infinite justice.*

Alongside the optimistic consensus of the 1990s, there emerged this more pessimistic view of human beings and human history, rooted in an interpretation of the Holocaust and deriving from it a deep pessimism. This view has been given impetus since September 11, 2001. Rancière observes that,

> Two traits characterize this ethical turn. It is above all a reversal of the course of time: time turned toward an end to be realized – progress, emancipation, or otherwise – is replaced by time turned toward the catastrophe that lies behind us. But it is also a leveling of the forms themselves of catastrophe. The extermination of the Jews appears then as the manifest form of a global situation that characterizes as well our democratic, liberal existence . . . This appears then as the accomplishment of an ontological destiny that allows no place for political dissensus.[25]

The appropriation of this perspective by the Bush administration in the post-9/11 war on terror is manifest (although it is unlikely that administration officials reflected on recent theoretical interpretations of the Holocaust). The war on terror is not like other wars. Its enemy is not readily identifiable, is not confined to any particular geographical area, does not depend on or give allegiance to a particular political system, cannot sign treaties or signal surrender, and so on. The enemy is everywhere and always threatening. The struggle against it is without borders and without end. It is more like the struggle of the good Christian against Satan than the secular wars characteristic of human history. And, like Satan, it is an evil that can appear within us – within the body politic or the body itself – as well as outside.

> The war against terror and infinite justice fall then into the indistinction of a preventative justice that blames everything that sustains or is capable of sustaining terror, everything that menaces the social

> bond that binds a community. It is a justice whose logic can only allow cessation when terror ceases, which, by definition, can never cease for those beings submitted to the trauma of birth. It is, in the same gesture, a justice to which no other justice can serve as a norm, a justice which is placed beyond all rule of right.[26]

If evil is everywhere threatening, it must be combated everywhere. And because it is evil, the struggle against it answers to no normative constraints. This formula justifies not only intervention into other countries, but also minute surveillance into one's own population. There are no rights that can override the war against terror, which is why the Bush administration can answer every charge brought against it for invasion of privacy, violation of rights, abusive treatment of detainees, neglect of the interests of allies, disdain for international agreements, with the same reply: we are saving lives and protecting our way of life. It is also, ironically, why the Islamic fundamentalists can engage in much the same behavior, with much the same high-handedness and disdain, and with almost exactly the same reply: we are saving the lives and the life of Islam. In both cases, the neglect of moral limits is justified by the struggle against pervasive evil and the preservation of a way of life that that evil threatens.

The emergence of ethics (in Rancière's idiomatic use of the term, as distinguished from our use of it in the previous chapter) in the post-9/11 world does not preclude the earlier neoliberal consensus model of the 1990s, in Europe or the U.S. Although it removes the optimism associated with the consensus model, in two other ways ethics reinforces it. First, what terrorism aims at is what has been called *our way of life*. That way of life is defined by capitalism and liberal freedom. The struggle against terrorism is waged on behalf of a historical legacy of markets and, to one degree or another, individualism and personal liberty. Neoliberalism is, centrally, the object to be protected in the war on terrorism.

Moreover, the war on terrorism requires consensus. This is the second way ethics reinforces the consensus model. There can be no dissensus in this war. Opposition to the war on terror, whether to its concept or its methods, is inevitably a form of giving aid and comfort to the terrorists themselves. In a speech before Congress nine days after September 11, President Bush laid out a framework that remains with us: either you are with us or you are with the terrorists.[27] There is no other political ground. If one is not in consensus with those struggling against terrorism, one is on the other side. This is Rancière's concept of the police in its most simple and stark form.

While distinct from the consensus model of the 1990s in substituting fear for optimism, the war on terror reinforces both the neoliberalism and the necessity of consensus characteristic of the earlier model. That is why it has not so much replaced the consensus model as arisen alongside and, more recently, subsumed it.

Of course, this subsumption has not been entirely without effects on the model itself. The pessimism of ethics has infused the neoliberal model as well, casting a pall over the consumerism it promotes. Rancière observes that in recent discussions in Europe, this consumerism is said to be a sign of an individualism gone amok, an unlimited degree of personal expression whose touchstone is the chaos of the 1960s. This introduces an ambivalence into the privileging of "democracy" that has been the cornerstone of Western self-justification. As Rancière puts it, the formula for this pessimism is

> Democratic government . . . is bad when it is allowed to be corrupted by a democratic society that wants everyone to be equal and all differences to be respected. It is good, on the other hand, when it recalls the flabby individuals of that democratic society to the energy of the war for the defense of values of civilization, which are those of the struggle of civilizations [i.e. the war against Islamic terrorism].[28]

He sums up this recent suspicion regarding democratic individualism as a

> triple operation: it is necessary, first, to reduce democracy to a form of society; second, to identify this form of society with the reign of egalitarian individualism, subsuming under this concept all sorts of disparate properties from rampant consumerism to claims of minority rights, passing along the way trade union struggles; and finally, to cash out (*verser au compte*) the "individualist society of the masses" thus identified with democracy in the quest for an indefinite growth that is inherent in the logic of the capitalist economy.[29]

The result of this triple operation is a contemporary interpretation of equality and a new form of inequality as a response to it. Equality is interpreted as a leveling of values resulting from capitalist consumerism. This leveling leaves no distinctions among the better and the worse, and gives everyone license to press what seem to be endless claims for recognition or assistance. The inequality responding to this is a renewed distrust of the people, the demos. Since the people are driven by the base materialist needs promoted by consumer society, they are unworthy, not only of the recognition they seek, but of governing the society they live in.[30]

This ambivalence about democracy has its resonance in the United States, particularly among those aligned with the religious right. Their critique of materialism, whether in its consumerist guise or its appearance in the theory of natural selection, reflects a concern with the effects of individual expression and an unconstrained freedom. By reducing all values into market values, everything becomes a matter of personal choice. The distinction between higher, sacred values and lower ones is lost. With this loss come the attendant losses of spirituality, family values, and the importance of tradition. It is this thread that ties together the disparate critiques of gay marriage, evolutionary theory, abortion, and affirmative action. All of these reflect, in one way or another, an orientation toward materialism and personal satisfaction at the expense of the distinction between the higher and the lower characteristic of traditional religion.

One might pause here over a seeming conflict between this pessimistic attitude toward democracy defined in terms of individualism and consumerism and the support for an unrestrained capitalism that circulates through the same schools of thought. In Rancière's eyes, the European model is not contradictory because, while it supports capitalism, it also supports an oligarchy that oversees capitalism's operation. This is the technocracy we saw above. Recall that the European approach to global capitalism is filtered through the regulation of the European Union, so that its operation and effects are overseen by an elite body. In the U.S., on the other hand, since the commitment to markets and the suspicion of government is more deeply rooted, there is more internal tension.

It appears in the Republican Party in the conflict between those who favor free markets and the social conservatives of the religious right. Although both oppose what they commonly refer to as "big government," they differ on whether issues like abortion, gay rights, flag burning, and, in some cases, drugs,[31] should be subject to legislation. For the free market wing of the Republican Party, whose base is in the Northeast and the West Coast, the market should decide these issues, not political legislation. Those who want abortions should have them, if there are others who want to provide them. Likewise, flag burning is for those who like to burn flags, and gays should have the same rights as all others. For social conservatives, however, who are the currently ascendant wing of the party, the liberty endorsed by free market conservatives is dangerous. Although in some general sense opposed to government intervention into the operations of the market, they favor specific social legislation, legislation that would restore the values the market seems to have either neglected or effaced. It is not always clear that this position is coherent, although in assigning blame for the purported demise of values, the focus has generally been on a culture of liberalism rather than on the economic mechanisms of capitalism.

Regardless of the theoretical coherence of these various positions, they converge on a resistance to democratic politics. The consensual model regards the dissensus of a democratic politics to be retrograde. Those who resist global capitalism inhabit a world that has passed them by; they refuse to accommodate themselves to a new order in which there is a place for everyone. Their exemplary figure of resistance, particularly in Europe, is that of the skinhead: angry, xenophobic, aimless. To the racism and provincialism of the past, global capitalists oppose a new economic order beyond political divisions. For them, politics is a matter of management and administration, not division and dissent.

The ethical turn is no less a project of suppressing a democratic politics, but in a more sober way. The pervasiveness of evil gives the lie to any trust in the people. The Holocaust is a sign that humans tend toward one of two camps: executioners or victims. "All differences are thus effaced before the law of a global situation. This appears then as the accomplishment of an ontological destiny that leaves no place for political dissensus, and can only await the safety of an improbable ontological revolution."[32] The solidarity required by a democratic politics must be submerged in favor of state projects of confronting evil, that is to say the war on terror. Dissensus is dangerous; it puts one closer to the side of evil. Until the improbable ontological revolution, which means until humans are different from what they are, the flirtation with hope characteristic of a democratic politics is in actuality an invitation to disaster. "[T]oday evil . . . has become the trauma that knows neither innocent nor guilty; it is a state of indistinction between culpability and innocence, between illness of the spirit and social trouble."[33] Combined with a distrust of the people that stems from their attachment to materialism and consumerism, the ethics of evil leaves no space for the sharing, trust, or dissensus characteristic of a democratic politics.

These, then, are the obstacles Rancière sees facing the formation of a democratic politics today. Are there lessons to be had here about democratic organizing in the face of these obstacles? Can we draw at least some tentative conclusions that will allow us to situate democratic politics in the current situation without betraying the requirement that such a politics must come from the demos rather than being imposed upon it?

There are at least four lessons. The first two concern the obstacles that lie in the way of *presupposing* equality; the latter two concern obstacles to *acting* on that presupposition.

The first obstacle is that the framework of both consensus and ethics presuppose inequality. The consensus model does so straight-forwardly. The consensus required by the European Union is not a consensus of the people. It has no affinities with the kind of discourse ethics proposed by thinkers like Habermas. It does not involve coming to a consensus at all. Rather, it concerns signing onto a consensus that has been decided by the technocrats that determine the economic parameters of the union. There are those who know, those who are expert, those who, in France at least, come from the schools that provide the technological understanding that allows for a proper intervention into market mechanisms. For the rest, there is only to participate in the framework the technocrats construct. Consensus, in this sense, means something like: no dissensus. The opinions of the people are neither sought nor welcomed. What is asked of them only is that they recognize that there are others who know better than they do, and that they do not resist this fact. That is why, as Rancière points out, when the people do resist, as for instance when the French voted against the European Constitution in May, 2005, this is con-sidered not so much a matter of opposition as of ignorance.

We can be more specific. The inequality ascribed to the people is an ignorance about economics. In a world dominated by neoliberal-ism, those who are not conversant with the workings of the market need to yield their political involvement to those who are. Where pol-itics is a matter of proper economic administration, only those with economic expertise are qualified to participate fully in the political realm.

The proper response to this presupposed inequality is not to claim that everyone can understand economics, but instead to deny that politics is a matter of economic administration. Where politics is democratic, where it concerns people's expression of their equality, then the charge that they are not familiar with economic theory is mis-placed. This does not entail, of course, that ignorance of economics is to be embraced. To the contrary. Particularly in an epoch where pol-itics is often reduced to economics, it is worth having at least a passing familiarity with that to which politics is being reduced. However, the possession of such knowledge, while helpful for understanding our current situation, is hardly requisite for political participation. To claim that it is amounts to another attempt to close the door on a democratic politics. It is another way in which, as Rancière puts it, "The art of politics consists in suppressing the political."[34]

In the ethical realm, the appearance of the presupposition of inequality is only slightly more subtle. If evil lies everywhere, the project of creating a democratic politics faces two insuperable dangers. The first is that it is beyond the ability of a democratic politics to confront this evil. It must be faced by those who have the means and the ability to do so. We have already seen a convergence between this view and neoliberalism in President Bush's exhortation to Americans in the wake of 9/11 to shop. It has been widely remarked that this comment reflects a deeply consumerist turn in the United States, and has been lamented for not asking more of Americans. What is less often remarked is the presupposed inequality inherent in the comment. You shop; we will take care of the serious business of dealing with terrorists. Was this not the import, not only of a particular statement by the president, but of the entire trajectory of the current administration? And if this administration is particularly flagrant in its appeal to inequality, is the framework of its general approach really aberrant? There is great evil afoot, we are told, and it takes a political superiority in order to confront (if not master, because it cannot be mastered) this evil. We will do so; you just go about your business. It has been the mantra of many administrations before this. One might make the case that the Cold War served much this same purpose.

The other danger associated with a democratic politics confronting evil is that it is not only powerful but also pervasive. The implication of this is that the future of any political expression is unclear. The lesson of the twentieth century is that creations of politics in the name of the people are risky endeavors. They can wind up, as the case of the Soviet Union shows, in repressing what they meant to liberate. Or worse. Because we are enshrouded by evil, we cannot predict the outcome of political intervention, and particularly of radical political intervention. This is why politics can only have two forms: confrontation of evil by the powers of the state and humanitarian assistance by those not involved with the state. What these two forms converge upon, as we have seen, is the figure of the victim.

In the face of this challenge from ethics, one cannot deny the contingency of political expression. That one does not know the outcomes of one's practices is a truth to which Foucault and others have long called our attention, and we ignore it at our peril. We must remain vigilant about the effects of a democratic politics. There are no transcendental guarantees, no politics whose programs can be given in advance. "The society of equals," Rancière says, "is only the ensemble of egalitarian relations that are traced here and now across singular and precarious acts."[35] Our history should serve as a reminder of just how precarious those acts can be. But precariousness is not the same thing as evil. If there are no guarantees of success, neither are there guarantees of failure. Evil is not a pervasive feature of the world. It is an outcome of historically contingent acts and practices that are sometimes mistaken and sometimes cynical. The elites are no more immune to this than the rest of us. The lesson we should draw here is not that of abandoning politics in favor of humanitarian assistance (nor, of course, is it to deny that such assistance is ever required), but to remain self-reflective in our political expression, to understand its contingency and precariousness, and to be ready to change course when equality is threatened.

This obstacle, the presupposed inequality inherent in consensus and in ethics, is reflected from the other side of coin. It is not only the messages emanating from the political and economic elites that reinforce out political inequality and incapacity. They lie as well in the character of our daily practices. Our world is not only neoliberal in theory; it is also consumerist in practice. While, on the one hand, elites reinforce the idea of our presupposed inequality to them, on the other, we ratify that inequality in our own practices. The message that we should shop does not fall entirely on unwilling ears. The practices of a neoliberal world are of a piece with the messages those who have a part give to the rest of us.

To say this is not to ratify the view we discussed above, that the demos is inherently materialistic or individualistic. Rather, it is to recognize that, while we are not helplessly determined by our historical context, neither are we immune to it. We are built out of our daily practices, not only creating but also created by them.[36] Our political inertia, then, does not only stem from above in the words and acts of the elites (or, as discussed in Chapter 1, in the words of our theories). It also bubbles up from below in the consumerist practices of our current world. When malls replace the public market as gathering places; when universities, museums, and other places of culture are increasingly run by reference to economic efficiency; when we begin to think of our lives in terms of shopping, on the one hand, and of investments and returns of our time, on the other, then we become engaged in the economic perspective that reinforces a view of politics that excludes us from it.

This point entails another one. We have discussed it several times above and can only touch upon it here from another angle. We have seen that domination is multifarious in its forms. There is no particular class of elites, of those who have a part, and of those who do not. This does not mean, of course, that nobody is more culpable than anybody else when it comes to domination. Rather, it means that, say, relative to economic domination certain wealthier individuals are the part who have a part, while relative to gender domination most males are the part who have a part. If we recall this point in the context of the idea that our participation in daily practices helps reinforce the denial of equality, then we can begin to recognize how often we ourselves participate in the domination of one another. The factory worker who buys shoes from a company that exploits Third World labor is participating in a practice that, not only in regard to specific exploited workers but also in its contribution to the neoliberal economic order, helps buttress the message of inequality bound to that order.

This does not mean, of course, that the factory worker is just as responsible for the denial of equality as the factory owner, or the current political elites. What it means is that we are not only the objects of the denial of equality; we are, inevitably, its subjects as well.[37]

The first two lessons we have discussed concern obstacles to the presupposition of equality. They are ways in which the arrangements of the current world reinforce the message that the demos is indeed less than equal to those who govern them and the world they live in. The next two lessons, intimately bound to each other and to the first two, focus not so much on obstacles to presupposing oneself to be equal but upon acting on that presupposition. This distinction, of course, is a bit arbitrary, since if one cannot act on the presupposition of one's equality then one begins to wonder whether one is indeed as equal as one might have thought. However, the accent of these next two lessons is placed at a slightly different point. The first one is a familiar theme concerning fear. The second one, which we have already treated briefly, concerns hope.

The consensus model does not operate from a pretext of fear. But the ethical model does. It appeals to a fear of what one can neither see nor grasp, a fear not only of the other but also of oneself. The appeal to fear as a form of politics is hardly new.[38] However, its current operation is particularly dangerous for acting on the presupposition of equality. We have already seen that a democratic politics is considered inadequate for dealing with evil both because it is powerful and because it is pervasive. This evil, whose derivation stems in Rancière's view from a particular appropriation of the Holocaust but whose dominant current name is *terrorism*, has been invoked to paralyze any attempt to introduce democracy into politics. Speaking personally for a moment, I recall visiting my home town of New York City several weeks after the events of September, 2001. It was stunning, and more than a bit disheartening, to see the displays of fervent patriotism across a city that had always considered itself to be, in Spalding Gray's words, "an island off the coast of America."[39] It seemed to me then, and in retrospect seems more so, that the patriotic response of Americans to these events would do more to prevent our understanding them than any other response we could have had. As we now know, the current administration has never ceased to bind this patriotism to a politics of fear that has been more than effective in stifling dissent from its policies both foreign and domestic.

From the rising and falling of color-coded security threats to false claims of weapons of mass destruction and terrorist links to the attempt to smear anyone who questions policy decisions as a tool of the terrorists, the current U.S. administration has raised the politics of fear to a central mode of governance. This is not to deny that there are terrorists and practices of terrorism. To the contrary, what gives the administration's policies traction is the intermittent reinforcement they receive from real acts of terror. One could ask, of course, whether those policies actually help foster the actions they seek to prevent. However, our question lies elsewhere. What effects do the politics of fear have on the project of building a democratic politics?

Those effects are not far to seek. When people are fearful their first priority becomes security. They are less likely to engage in practices that make them vulnerable and more likely to withdraw from practices that do. That, of course, is what makes courage special. It lies in the ability to maintain one's practices when faced with a threat. However, during periods of hope the ability to sustain oneself in a situation of fear is augmented. When there is a significant goal in view, particularly a goal with deep meaning, combined with the belief that that goal is attainable, people are often more willing to persevere under threat of harm. In periods like those of the civil rights movement in the U.S., the anti-colonial struggles in Asia and Africa, or the labor rights movement of the late nineteenth and early twentieth centuries, hope provided a salve to ease fear. However, those periods are the exception. Ours is not characterized by struggles like these.

This is why, although the politics of fear is grounded in the ethical framework Rancière discusses, it is sustained by the consensus model of neoliberalism. The operation of fear is nourished by the denial of hope. More precisely, the consensus model, by defining hope in a certain way and denying all other forms of hope, sets the stage for the politics of fear to operate unchallenged.

"The consensus that governs us," Rancière writes, "is a machine of power insofar as it is a machine of vision. It pretends to verify only what everyone can see by adjusting two propositions on the state of the world: one which says that we are finally at peace, and the other which announces the condition of this peace: the recognition that there is only what there is."[40] Peace is the hope, the condition for which is the absence of any other hope: there is only what there is, and can be nothing else. What is this peace, and how does it require the abandonment of other forms of hope? It is a peace that is derived from the absence of conflict.

Consider this: corporations do not like to invest in areas of civil unrest. This is why they do not mind investing in countries with stable totalitarian governments, such as Pinochet's Chile or current China, but will not invest in places like the Congo or South Africa near the end of apartheid, where the political future is more unpredictable. Investment brings exactly the type of hope promised by neoliberalism: jobs and consumer goods. Neoliberal hope is economic. It does not find hope in the expression of equality but in the presence of material goods and the ability to purchase those goods. In fact, the dissensual character of the expression of equality makes it anathema to the hope neoliberalism promotes. The equation is this: neoliberalism = consensus = peace = jobs, security, and consumer goods. The other equation, the one to be avoided, is: democracy = dissensus = conflict = instability. Democratic politics is a recipe for disinvestment. Its threat of disorder is an invitation to capital flight.

Here is precisely where the politics of fear and the denial of hope converge. We can see it either from the side of ethics or from that of consensus. From the side of ethics, there is a threat that must be confronted, if not ever entirely defeated, and the persistence of this threat implies that the best one can hope for is a modicum of security and material well-being. From the side of consensus, there is an optimism that lies solely in the global development of the capitalist order, an optimism that requires for its achievement the end of any project of a democratic politics. Expressions of equality threaten this development, and therefore must be left to the margins of economic development. From either side, there is an extortion, one that arises not from (or not necessarily from) the attempt to extort, but from the framework in which politics is thought. There is no concerted conspiracy against a democratic politics, even if there may be the occasional conspirator. Instead, there are two political orientations, one optimistic and one pessimistic, whose point of intersection is the rejection of democracy. For one, democracy is a flirtation with evil and the introduction of insecurity; for the other, it is the injection of instability and a threat to investment. And in our world, the two work together in an uneasy yet powerful alliance.

They also work in concert with the first two obstacles we have discussed, that consensus and ethics both presuppose inequality and give rise to practices that allow us to presuppose our own inequality. There are two relations in particular that call for attention. The first is the way in which the presupposition of inequality reinforces fear. If the demos is indeed inferior to the elites who govern consensus or fight the war on terror, then the project of resistance becomes a source of fear. The feeling that one is less than equal to those one struggles against does not inspire confidence in the success of one's struggle. Rather, it inspires timidity. The inequality presupposed by the consensus and ethical models is intimidating to those who would dissent against them. In that way, they preserve their dominance.

The other relation is that between the practices we engage in and the types of hope we permit ourselves. We saw above that neoliberalism, with its emphasis on the economic, tempts us toward projects of material comfort. Consumerism stands in for practices of equality. It provides exactly the kind of hope that neoliberalism promotes: peace without dissensus. To the extent that we participate willingly in consumerist practices, we reinforce on a daily basis the belief that hope consists in what we can purchase rather than in the collective expression of equality we can achieve. It makes us into beings lacking the hope associated with a democratic politics.

How ought those who seek to construct a democratic politics respond to the promotion of fear and the denial of hope? We saw above that action in the face of fear is often best sustained during periods of hope. This suggests that, rather than diminishing fear directly, fortifying hope holds more promise. I believe this is the right approach. Telling someone not to be afraid does not strengthen them. It does not offer resolve. Giving them a reason to persist in the face of fear does. But this goes a very little way toward answering our question. Hope does not arise ex nihilo. It is not enough to advise someone to hope, without at least suggesting what can be hoped for. One cannot manufacture hope outside the context of the situations one finds oneself in. Are there reasons for hope at this moment in history, reasons that can respond to the convergence of consensus and ethics?

It is difficult to answer this question in general. The reasons that arise for hope often appear in response to local conditions and are shaped by them. One recent example of hope is the work of the Zapatistas in the indigenous areas of southern Mexico. The Zapatistas have inspired a sense of collective hope among people who have existed on the margins of Mexican society at least since its independence in the early part of the twentieth century. They have introduced not only structures of collective decision-making but also a sense that the traditional policies of Mexico's government, policies that disfavor indigenous peoples in particular, can be challenged. One might ask why it is that at a particular moment – January 1994, to be exact – indigenous people were willing to support an insurrection that had not seemed a possibility to them earlier. Part of the answer would lie in the deleterious effects of globalization on their economic situation. (The uprising of 1994 was timed to coincide with the moment NAFTA took effect.) But another important part of the explanation has to do with the type of organizing that was done. The Zapatistas did not simply impose an ideological framework on their organizing efforts. They sought to appeal to the beliefs and orientation of the people of Chiapas. They turned the culture of the indigenous people of southern Mexico – their symbols, their beliefs, the structure of their personal relationships – into a source of pride, and thus of hope.[41]

This example does not offer a formula for the appearance of hope. If anything, it moves in the opposite direction, showing why democratic hope has no formula. The lesson it imparts would be one of sensitivity to openings and possibilities that lie within particular conditions rather than seeking a general approach to resistance. For much of the sectarian left, this would be lesson enough. However, one might ask the question of whether, if there are no formulas for dissensus in this time period, there are at least some generalities that might help orient us.

I would like to respond to this question by proposing one that stems from my own experience as a college professor. I cannot establish how widespread this generality is, although my experience seems to point in the direction of its being at least fairly so. It concerns the orientation of my students. In recent years, more of them seem dissatisfied with their world. This dissatisfaction is inchoate, but might be marked by saying that the material comforts offered to them in their future prospects do not seem to be enough. As in the late 1960s, although much less pronounced and – because this is a different era – differently inflected, increasing numbers of students want something other than what neoliberalism has on offer. It might be said, at some risk of oversimplification, that increasing numbers of students are concerned that the world into which they are to be sent is boring. They would like something more meaningful than working at anonymous jobs in multinational corporations, eating at restaurant chains, and watching blockbuster movies or sporting event spectacles. While not actively seeking something else, they wonder whether this is all there is to their lives, whether, in Rancière's terms, there is only what there is.

As I have described it here, this does not look much like hope. I believe, however, that it is hope in its nascent stage. The students I am describing here are not in despair. While they do not know what they are looking for, they have at least that minimal degree of hope that consists in the belief that it is worth looking. And when, as I often do, I teach courses on various types of progressive theory, they are responsive. Not uncritical, and not without a measure of skepticism born of the context we have been describing here. But responsive nonetheless. I have seen this disquiet not only at my own university, but among students at other places I have spoken. It appears periodically in the brush fires of progressive politics that have emerged recently, particularly since the anti-globalization movement of the mid-1990s.

There is much arrayed against this hope, and students seem to sense it. They are more tentative than students a generation before them: more sober in expression and less likely to embrace more utopian visions. However, to the extent that they are willing to seek something more than consumerism as their hope for the future, they provide an audience open to the possibility of a democratic politics, either on their own behalf or in solidarity with others whose more desperate situation in the neoliberal order is a source of struggle.

So far, discussion has centered on the convergence of the consensus and ethical models Rancière discusses. We will turn now to the issue of globalization, although it is inseparable from the neoliberalism and the war on terror we have already addressed. We should note at the outset, however, that the concept of globalization is itself a source of conflict. In some sense, globalization has been going on at least since Europe starting sending out shipping expeditions in the 1400s. The colonialism that resulted from these expeditions was certainly a global affair. If the term is to be used in a historically-specific way, its reference must be to something other than the fact that there is global interaction.

What this historical specificity consists in is where the disagreement arises. For some, globalization lies in the rise of transnational capitalism and the demise of the nation-state.[42] The nation-state, itself a recent historical development, is being effaced by technological developments in communication that allow capitalism to operate without regard to national borders. The elites, according to this view, will be predominantly economic, with the political elites serving only in an adjunct capacity. Others, among them Antonio Negri and Michael Hardt in their book *Empire*,[43] while sympathetic to the idea of a rise of transnational capitalism, are not prepared to endorse the idea of a complete demise of the nation-state. Negri and Hardt see a three-tiered global system arising, one that has the U.S. and perhaps a few other wealthy nations on top, transnational corporations next, and non-governmental organizations at the third tier.

For his part, Rancière is wary of talk of the decline of the nation-state. He sees a dynamic between economic and political control at work in the form of what he calls, in his recent book *La haine de la démocratie*, an *oligarchy*. "To suppress national limits in favor of the unlimited expansion of capital, to submit the unlimited expansion of capital to national limits: in the conjunction of these two tasks is defined the final figure of the royal science."[44] The oligarchy consists in those who manage the global system in such a way as to prevent dissensus. They are indispensable to the current global order. "The ineluctable historical necessity is in fact only the conjunction of two proper necessities: one, the unlimited growth of wealth; the other, the growth of oligarchical power . . . The same states that abdicate their privileges before the free circulation of capital recover them in order to close their borders to the free circulation of the planet's poor in search of work."[45]

The precise role of the nation-state in the formation and sustaining of globalization need not detain us here. What these different views allow are at least three characteristics to globalization. First, there is an expansion of corporate power across borders, an expansion that we have discussed already under the heading of neoliberalism. Second, regardless of the specific role national borders play, there has been an increased porousness of national borders that is reflected in both a mobility of populations and a fragility of many national entities. Finally, and related, improvements in communication technologies offer increased virtual interaction among far-flung parts of the world. Without these improvements, the expansion of capital and the mobility of populations would be far slower than it is. Conversely, this expansion and mobility has motivated the development of communication technology. Whether the dynamic between corporate expansion, the porousness of borders, and technological development is continuous with earlier forms of globalization or constitutes an entirely new global order does not concern us. (Although it is undoubtedly happening at a faster pace than previously.) What does concern us is its relevance for democratic politics.

We have seen already that the expansion of capitalism has erected new obstacles in the way of democratic political organizing. What about the second characteristic: the porousness of borders, the mobility of populations, and the fragility of certain states? Rancière points out that a mobile population does not necessarily include those who have no part. Recently in the U.S., and for some time in Europe, debates over immigration have stirred concern precisely over the issue of borders. These debates do not bear upon the elites who seek to enter a country. It is not doctors and engineers who are the topic of discussion. It is the lower classes, those who seek to escape an impoverished or repressive existence, who find themselves subject to these (often racially tinged) disagreements.

Further, it is the same people who are living in, and thus trying to leave, fragile or failed states. Mexico, the Central American countries, Algeria, Mali: these are the places from which many of the immigrants arrive. They are not protected in their own countries, and either denied entry or largely unprotected in the countries in which they seek shelter or work. Here one can see clearly the failure of the humanitarian strategy in addressing the problems at hand. Humanitarianism does not begin, nor does it see itself as attempting, to address the political problem confronting those who become immigrants. Neither inequality nor political action is its concerns. By turning them into victims, the humanitarian strategy denies their democratic political potential. For humanitarianism, these people are not equals. They cannot be, because they exist solely as recipients, while the donors exist solely as actors.

In a recent discussion, Rancière shows how the concept of human rights, which is central to the humanitarian strategy, reinforces the anti-political character of such a strategy. One would think that the idea of human rights would be more nearly political. After all, it concerns claims that humans, as humans, can make upon their governments. The idea of a human right is that of a right that people *ought* to be protected in, even when in fact they are not. That *ought* can be used as a springboard for action, and has been, most prominently by groups like Amnesty International and Human Rights Watch. And, no doubt, intervention by these groups has served to mitigate some of the horrors of more oppressive political regimes. However, there are at least two elements to the framework of human rights that deflect it from a more political path. The first, just mentioned, is that it turns its objects into victims. The second, Rancière argues, is that it plays into a certain kind of interventionism by more powerful states.

Rancière starts his discussion of this interventionism by calling to mind Hannah Arendt's own treatment of human rights. In *The Origins of Totalitarianism*, she argues that rights can only occur within the context of a polity. "The Rights of Man, after all, had been defined as 'inalienable' because they were supposed to be independent of all governments; but it turned out that the moment human beings lacked their own government and had to fall back on their minimum rights, no authority was left to protect them and no institution was willing to guarantee them."[46] In her view, the tragedy that visited much of humanity in the twentieth century was not that people's rights were not guaranteed, but rather the absence of a development of polities in which those rights *could be* guaranteed. "Not the loss of specific rights, then, but the loss of a community willing and able to guarantee any rights whatsoever, has been the calamity which has befallen ever-increasing numbers of people."[47]

In Rancière's view, the shift from Arendt's Rights of Man to humanitarianism reflects the rise of the consensus model. Because of its commitment to neoliberalism and depoliticization, consensus does not work by shoring up the polities whose absence Arendt laments. (This, of course, would not be Rancière's recommendation either, but for very different reasons.) Instead, the consensus model accords everyone rights. However, those for whom humanitarian rights seem to matter are those who cannot press them on their own behalf. "[T]he Rights of Man become the rights of those who have no rights, the rights of bare human beings subjected to inhuman repression and inhuman conditions of existence."[48] This would seem like an empty conception of rights. Everyone has rights; it is just that some people, an increasing number in our globalized world, are unfortunate enough not to be able to realize them.

However, this conception of rights is not politically inert. Immediately following the words just cited, Rancière writes, "They become humanitarian rights, the rights of those who cannot enact them, the victims of the absolute denial of rights. For all this, they are not void. The void is filled by somebody or something else. The Rights of Man do not become void by becoming the rights of those who cannot actualize them. If they are not truly 'their' rights, they can become the rights of others."[49] To whom do these rights revert? To the granter of the rights, to those who claim their existence in the first place. They devolve upon those whose rights are protected by intact polities, that is, to the powerful. And how do these rights appear? As the right of intervention on behalf of the victim of the denial of rights.

We have seen this strategy in action over the past dozen years. It appeared in the interventions into Somalia, Bosnia, Kosovo, and more recently Iraq. It should be emphasized that it is not being claimed here that there is no role for intervention to play. One might make a strong argument that in at least one instance, that of Rwanda, the problem was a *failure* of intervention. What is at issue here is not the justifiable of this or that intervention, but rather the framework within which intervention is considered. This framework operates by denying the democratic political potential of those in whose name intervention occurs. Intervention becomes a matter of protecting the human rights of those who are nothing more than those rights. It coincides with a view that those who have no part are mere victims, and therefore are less than equal to those who have a part. In this sense, interventionism and the treatment of people as victims are two sides of the same coin. If the objects of the humanitarian strategy are nothing more than victims, they will be unable to create or express any form of equality. Ensuring their minimally decent treatment requires intervention from the outside, from a group or a state that is capable of more than passive suffering.

Moreover, this coincidence also converges with a consensus model that, by treating people as victims, forecloses the possibility of dissensus. The problem is not that some people are less equal; it is that not everyone has access to the peaceful workings of the global capitalist market. The point of intervention is not solidarity with those who struggle against the politics of inequality. It is instead to bring the intervened upon into what is often called "the community of nations," by which is meant the current global order.

The humanitarian strategy, in addition to intersecting with the neoliberal consensus model, reinforces the more recent ethical model. This model, more pessimistic than the consensus model, sees a pervasive evil that must always be confronted by superior state force. We have seen that the ethical model, convergent with the humanitarian strategy, sees people as victims and worries that their attempt to become active rather than passive will result in their promoting evil. Thus, the evil that has been done to these victims must be addressed not by the people themselves but by the powers that arrogate to themselves an intervention based upon the human rights of their objects. Recalling the abandoned term *infinite justice* that President Bush used to characterize the war on terror, Rancière writes,

> An infinite justice is not only a justice that dismisses the principles of International Law, prohibiting interference with the "internal affairs" of another state; it is a justice which erases all distinctions that used to define the field of justice in general: the distinctions between law and fact, legal punishment and private retaliation, justice, police, and war. All those distinctions are boiled down to a sheer ethical conflict between Good and Evil.[50]

How might a democratic politics address the humanitarian strategy? Does it need to abandon all its elements – victimization, interventionism, and human rights – or can some aspect of it be maintained? Certainly, the first two elements must be jettisoned. Victimization allows, at best, passive equality. The construction of an active equality that is the project of a democratic politics moves in precisely the opposite direction. Interventionism must also be abandoned. This does not entail that intervention is never justified. What it does entail is that intervention cannot by itself be seen as an aspect of an emancipatory politics. For the idea of interventionism must be substituted that of solidarity as we have defined it in the previous chapters. Struggle must be made alongside people rather than on their behalf. Perhaps, at certain extreme points, this may require an intervention. But if so, it must be done alongside those whom it supports rather than in their stead. And to do this, we must think of those alongside whom struggle occurs as equals and participants rather than victims. The coin with the two faces of victimization and interventionism must be re-minted.

One will surely point out that there are cases that might call for intervention where there is nobody alongside whom struggle can occur. In the case of Darfur in Sudan, for example, there is a victimization that seems to require intervention, but no indigenous group engaged in resistance that would be a natural building block for solidarity. This is a sad truth that cannot be denied. In a world where politics is framed by the humanitarian strategy, it is increasingly so. Even in situations like these, however, situations without a basis for democratic solidarity, we must still embrace a democratic orientation. We must look for openings for democratic expression that can be encouraged, and refuse to think of those on whose behalf one intervenes as victims. That is to say, even when intervention is required in a context without the current possibility of developing democratic solidarity, one must resist the temptations of the humanitarian strategy.

What about human rights, the third element of the humanitarian strategy? Must it be abandoned by any project of a democratic politics? I believe the situation here is more complicated. There seems to be no bar to prising apart the concept of human rights from that of the victim/interventionism complex into which it has been woven. To the contrary, the idea of rights can be an intimate part of democratic struggle. The right to equality, for instance, can be invoked not simply as a right to be granted by an institutional structure but a right that is expressed by a democratic politics. There can be other rights demanded as well. The French tailors' strike discussed in Chapter 2 can be seen in terms of a right to a wage commensurate with the equality of the tailors to their bosses. In discussing the campaign for equal rights for women in the French Revolution, Rancière argues that,

> Women could make a twofold demonstration. They could demonstrate that they were deprived of the rights that they had, thanks to the Declaration of Rights. And they could demonstrate, through their public action, that they had the rights that the constitution denied to them, that they could enact those rights.[51]

One of the reasons the concept of rights could be effective is that it contains the implication of universality discussed in Chapter 4. The invocation of rights, then, can be an invocation of universal equality. However, in order for there to be active equality, this invocation must be done primarily by those whose equality is being denied. It is in their expression of their rights, through their "public action," that rights become elements in a political strategy of equality, rather than when their stated rights revert to the powerful as a justification for intervention on their behalf.

Let us turn to the third element of globalization, the development of communication technologies. Here the situation is more complex.

It is not, as with neoliberalism and the humanitarian strategy, simply a matter of obstacles. On the one hand, these technologies have several deleterious effects on democratic politics. In addition to their role in supporting the expansion of transnational capitalism, they also allow for greater coordination among and infiltration by political elites in surveiling and taming populations. As I write this, there are debates in the U.S. on recent governmental recording of domestic telephone calls and gathering information on citizens such as library use, and in Britain concerning the ubiquity of public surveillance cameras and the collecting of private information on cards used for public transport. On the other hand, the rise of alternative media on the internet such as indymedia[52] has provided a source of information and organizing tools previously inaccessible to large groups of people. Information that would be inconvenient to the mainstream, often corporate-owned media can be posted on the internet and available to people who would otherwise lack access to it. In addition, organizing increasingly happens with the internet, allowing people who would otherwise not know each other to gather for demonstrations or other public actions.

One example of this is Critical Mass, bicyclists who gather together to ride through city streets, asserting both their rights to the road and the urgency of environmental awareness. The operation of Critical Mass is democratic. First, their slogan, *We aren't blocking traffic, we are traffic*, is an expression of equality. Bicyclists arrogate to their collective activity the equal right to be on publicly funded roads. Second, the self-organizing character of the rides, which often arise through the internet and through cell phones, allows them to maintain the presupposition of equality internally as well as externally. Critical Mass gatherings operate largely on sharing and trust, especially since they often encounter angry resistance from motorists and city officials.[53]

The rise of communication technologies, unlike neoliberalism and humanitarianism, is not connected to a specific political, economic, or conceptual framework. These technologies can intersect with practices that are both oppressive and emancipatory. Because of this, a democratic politics needs neither to embrace these technologies wholesale nor reject them. What a democratic politics can do is utilize them with a recognition of both the opportunities and dangers these technologies present. In particular, since these technologies bring people in contact with others at a geographic and cultural distance, a democratic politics must be vigilant about the presuppositions under which this contact is unfolding.

One point of vigilance, although obvious at a general level, is easy to overlook in the work of organizing. We have seen it already briefly, but it must be stressed particularly in the work of international solidarity. Those of us in economically and politically dominant countries must see ourselves struggling alongside those in other countries, not simply on their behalf. We cannot dictate to them where their oppression lies, nor articulate their experience for them as though they were incapable of articulating it themselves. To put the point another way, we cannot be the intellectuals to their proletariat.

This does not mean, as we saw in Chapter 4, that those who organize have nothing to say about the experience of others, or that in some cases people in developing countries may be mistaken about the source or structure of their oppression. Dialogue about these matters is not precluded. One is not reduced to listening to them and applauding their words. What it means is that when there is disagreement all must recognize the equality of those who struggle. One must speak with them rather than for them. To treat those in developing countries either as ignorant of their oppression or, in an inversion, as the only spokespeople for it – as radical chic – is to refuse them equality. We must act out of the presupposition of equality, both theirs and ours, and have our dialogue and our solidarity work proceed from there.

There is another lesson as well. Whatever differences there are in the experiences of those in the developed and the developing countries, whatever the divergences in viewpoints or perspectives, there is something we all share. We all face the same adversaries, and those adversaries – whether they are political institutions or multinational corporations – seek to remove us from participating in the formation of the shape of our world. They seek to treat us all as, in Rancière's words, a part that has no part. They seek to ensure that our words are ignored, our experience neglected, our actions silenced. Alongside those in developing countries, we in the developed countries face the same refusal of equality. Even more so as the world becomes increasingly globalized. That presents us with our challenge and our opportunity.

If we are to engage in an effective politics in solidarity with those in other countries, we need to structure our work around the same principles and strive toward complementary ends. Among those principles, and perhaps most prominent among them, stands the presupposition of equality. Armed with that presupposition, we can coordinate our work, discuss our similarities and our differences, form our sense of unity, and together face those for whom globalization is not a matter of equality but simply the chance to generalize domination.

The final stage of this discussion concerns the institutionalization of a democratic politics. Can democracy be institutionalized, or is it destined to remain a scattered and temporary? When we ask this question, we need not privilege any form or conception of institutionalization. At stake is not whether a democratic politics must take this or that particular form, but whether a democratic politics can yield permanent, or at least ongoing, structures of public space. Can the space of our collective lives, to one degree or another, be structured by the presupposition of equality, beyond the role that presupposition plays in our struggles against a particular police order?

This may seem a puzzling question to raise at this stage. We have been concerned here, more than in previous chapters, with the present state of things. The question of institutionalization is not situated solely in the present. It can be raised – and has been – under a variety of historical circumstances. What is its role in a reflection on democratic politics in the present?

The question of institutionalization is not so much of the present as of the future. It bears upon the character of what we can hope for from a democratic politics. So far, the conception of democratic politics that has been proposed treats it in the context of *resistance*. A democratic politics, in the present but also in the past, is a dissensus from the police order. But this dissensus is not simply reactive. It does not amount only to a refusal of the police order. It is, more significantly, an expression – the expression of equality. It is not, then, simply parasitical upon that from which it dissents. And because of this, one can ask about the eventual trajectory of this dissensus. Can a democratic politics loosen itself from a police order to the extent of creating its own space, a space where there is no police order? Can it go that far? Or must there always be a police order from which it dissents? If a democratic politics is not bound to be reactive to a given police order, is it circumscribed by the fact of having to arise within the context of *some* police order?

We can put the question another way, one that requires care if it is not to be misunderstood: can a democratic politics be revolutionary, or is it fated to remain reformist? If we put matters this way, we must recognize that the term revolutionary has a specific, and circumscribed, meaning. We cannot align the term with visions of utopia, for two related reasons. First, recall that democratic politics responds to domination, and domination happens not at a particular point but across a number of registers. To address a particular form of domination is not to address domination per se. It might be, for instance, that gays could act out of their own equality to the point where there was no domination of gays. This would be revolutionary in the sense of the term I am appealing to here, but it would not result in a utopia. It would not necessarily alter the inequalities suffered by women or immigrants.

Second, since domination happens across a number of registers and along a variety of fronts, the effects of different forms of resistance are uncertain. The contingencies of history that have so concerned Foucault apply as much to a democratic politics as to anything else. Given the complexity of dominations, what guarantee do we have that the results of a democratic politics in one area will not result in a new form of domination arising in another? None at all. We must, then, either jettison the term *revolutionary* or, alternatively, abandon the connection between that term and the idea of utopia. That things can get better is undeniable. That there is an ultimate state toward which democratic political struggle is oriented, aside from that of expressions of equality (or, alternatively put, ending various types of domination), is more doubtful.

To be wary of utopia, however, does not require us to surrender the possibility of institutionalizing a democratic politics. The question is not whether we will arrive at an ultimate state without any domination, but whether, among our particular – if often intersecting – struggles, it is conceivable that some will take on a more permanent character and will thus provide positive instances of living in equality, divorced from the dominations that previously characterized them.

Rancière is very clear on this question.

> The community of equals can always be realized, but only on two conditions. First, it is not a goal to be reached but a supposition to be posited from the outset and endlessly reposited . . . The second condition, which is much like the first, may be expressed as follows: the community of equals can never achieve substantial form as a social institution . . . A community of equals can never become coextensive with a society of the unequal, but nor can either exist without the other . . . A community of equals is an insubstantial community of individuals engaged in the ongoing creation of equality. Anything else paraded under this banner is either a trick, a school, or a military unit.[54]

For Rancière, there can be no institutionalization of a democratic politics. Democracy always occurs within the context of a police order.

One might argue here that this passage should be taken not as a rejection of institutionalization, but only of utopia. What Rancière is doing, it might be said, is refusing only that there can be an entire society of equals, which amounts to no more than saying that one cannot overcome *all* forms of domination. Is this nothing else than what we have just stated? If this were what Rancière was saying, it would still be different from the rejection of utopia we have just offered. The reason is that for Rancière the problem is that a community of equals *cannot exist* without a community of unequals in which it arises. The equal requires the unequal *in principle*. For us, by contrast, the problem is not one of principle but of complexity. It is because of the multiplicity of dominations that the appeal to utopia seems misplaced and even dangerous. The argument is not that there cannot be a democratic political utopia, but that to envision one in any specificity (that is, aside from the general idea of expressing equality) neglects both the various registers along which domination operates and the contingency that characterizes political struggle. Moreover, envisioning utopia invites the temptation to reduce a variety of dominations to one or two central ones that, when solved, pave the way for its realization. The twentieth century can stand as an object lesson for what happens when one yields to that temptation.

Rancière, however, is not simply rejecting utopia. His problem is not the narrow one of whether an entire society can be predicated on equality. He is rejecting the institutionalization of equality more generally. This is indicated by his use of the terms *substantial* and *insubstantial form* (in French, *consistance* and *inconsistante*). The community of equals is a subjectification that cannot achieve an institutional form without betraying itself as a community of equals. It is, instead, an insubstantial community that is both a dissensus from and bound to the police order in which it arises.

I believe Rancière has overstated the case here. But before saying why, it should be recognized that there is a consistency to his thought at this point. If a democratic politics is a dissensus, then it would seem to follow that there is something it is dissenting from. That something is, of course, a police order, a community of unequals. As we have seen, the fact of dissensus does not require that democratic politics be reactive. What Rancière indicates with the term *dissensus* is not the form of democratic politics itself, but the context within which it takes place. The expression of equality always occurs within a context of inequality. Whether that expression places demands upon those who have a part in that context is another, if related, issue. Given the character of police orders, most democratic politics will place such demands. However, they are defined not by the demands themselves but by the expression of equality out of which those demands arise.

The question I want to pose to Rancière's thought is not whether all democratic politics must arise within a context of inequality, a context that requires that it be a dissensus. This seems unavoidable. If there were no police order, there would be no motivation for a democratic politics in the first place. The question instead concerns the trajectory of such a politics. Is it possible for a dissensus that arises as a struggle within a police order to carry itself forward into a more substantial form without *necessarily* losing its character as an expression of equality? Must it be the case, in principle, that a democratic politics *cannot exist* without a police order?

It seems to me that a democratic politics does not need to be committed to that. Nor is it a requirement on Rancière's thought. Although the motivation for Rancière's claim is clear, the best position to take on the question of institutionalization is one of neutrality. As we said before, better agnostic than atheist on this question.

There seem to me to be two reasons for agnosticism. The first is that it fits the framework of Rancière's own thought better. In general, his thought moves outside the ambit of *in principle* commitments. This is in keeping with a particular intellectual modesty consistent with his larger view. In his rejection of Althusser's distinction between intellectuals and the masses, Rancière eliminates the role of the intellectual as the one who articulates the character of political struggle from on high. People are equally intelligent. They do not need an intellectual master to direct political struggle. In fact, if domination is as multiple and varied as Rancière's thought allows, then it is difficult to imagine how it could be overseen. But if the direction of a democratic politics cannot be overseen, how does one know where it will lead? By denying in advance that it can lead away from a police order altogether, Rancière seems to slip into an intellectual role that he is elsewhere careful to avoid.

One might want to say in his defense that the institutionalization of a democratic politics would no longer be a politics in Rancière's sense because, by definition, politics is a dissensus. Therefore, anything that moves beyond dissensus is no longer a form of politics. I don't think the term *community of equals* as it is used in the passage above lends itself to this interpretation, but in any case there is nothing at stake here. If we want to define a democratic politics as a dissensus, then the question we are raising is whether a democratic politics can lead to something else, whatever name we want to give it, that institutionalizes the presupposition of equality. Otherwise put, the question is whether a democratic politics can itself build institutions. I prefer the second formulation, because in order for the institutionalization really to be an expression of equality, it must arise from within a democratic struggle. As we have seen, passive equality is not the rich equality of a democratic politics. The second formulation recognizes the continuity of institution with struggle. However, there is no substantive distinction here between formulations.

The second reason for agnosticism has to do less with theoretical coherence and more with epistemic limitations. We just don't know where democratic politics can lead, and therefore cannot say with any confidence whether or not institutions can arise from democratic struggle. Rancière himself has provided the tools for constructing at least the possibility of institutionalization with the terms *sharing* and *trust*. Recall that the internal ethics of a democratic politics relies on the ability of its participants to share with and to trust one another. The relationships formed from sharing and trust are part of the glue that holds a democratic movement together. This glue contrasts with that which binds the individuals of many traditional institutions.

For example, contrast a democratic politics with the institution of work as it is in the current world. Both are characterized by a purpose that motivates the participants. In the first case it is the expression of equality, in the second the provision of some good or service. Without these purposes, neither would exist. However, in the case of work, there needs to be more to motivate people. In most cases, that *more* is money. What keeps people coming back to work every day is not only the good or service that is being provided. In fact, it is rarely that. For most working people, participation in creating the good or service is nearly irrelevant as a motivation. One works because one is paid. Although there are those whose work provides more intrinsic rewards, they are a small minority among the people who get up every morning and trudge off to their jobs.[55]

With a democratic politics, sharing and trust fill much of the role played by money at most jobs. To be sure, people participate in such a politics in part because of the specific goals to be attained and the expression of equality involved. However, the relationships that are developed in the course of political struggle, above and beyond the purposes of the movement, serve to keep people together. They motivate people to donate their time, to engage in boring and repetitive tasks, and often to make themselves vulnerable to verbal and, at times, physical abuse.

One might object here that one cannot base a set of social arrangements on sharing and trust. After all, people have to be paid somehow, or else they cannot continue to exist. Goods and services have to be provided. People will not provide them on the basis of sharing and trust alone. Those may be good for temporary political movements, but one cannot ground many of the ongoing institutions society requires on them.

The response to this objection is twofold. First, it must be granted that goods and services have to be provided in a society and that people have to have access to them. Moreover, the most likely way for these two things to happen is for the people who have access to them to be the same people as those who provide them. There is nothing in this, however, that precludes at the outset the integration of sharing and trust into whatever arrangements are made for this provision. If these elements could be integrated into the workplace, then it would seem that there would be more rather than less motivation to participate in work. And what goes for work also goes for other institutional forms, such as political and civic institutions. Even more so, since they often involve a good degree of voluntary participation.

Moreover, and this is the second part of the response, there are numerous instances of sharing and trust operating in contemporary society. Because of the liberal – and now neoliberal – ideology of individualism, especially in the U.S., we are often blind to them. But they exist nevertheless. On an informal level, friendships, which are rarely the object of philosophical reflection, are an arena largely defined by sharing and trust.[56] While not institutional, friendships tend to be ongoing. One's friendships often last longer over the course of a life than one's participation in any of one's jobs. It might be argued that friendships required an interpersonal cultivation that is not characteristic of many institutional forms, such as work. But we must ask whether this indicates some inescapable limit on friendship or instead the poverty of many of our institutional relationships.

Beyond friendship, there are other, more informal types of institutional relationships based on sharing and trust. Voluntary organizations, whether they be civic or recreational, are built both upon the purposes they serve and the relationships that are developed within them. Who returns to a bowling league or a soup kitchen week after week unless there are meaningful relationships to which people are drawn? Vibrant societies are replete with various institutions whose participation is a source of significant relationships for those involved. In fact, some thinkers, most notably Robert Putnam in *Bowling Alone*,[57] have argued that a society where these more informal institutions are lacking is a society in decline.

All we have done here, it will be claimed, is gesture at the role sharing and trust might play in the ongoing institutional arrangements of a society. We have not offered a program or even a specific framework for the realization of democratic institutions. We have not shown how an institution can grow organically out of democratic expression. All of this amounts to little more than a denial of a denial: a denial of Rancière's denial that a democratic politics can take a *substantial form*.

Indeed that is all that we have done. A denial of a denial, and a gesture toward the possibilities of sharing and trust. Theoretically, that is all that can be done. What we have tried to accomplish is to keep the door open to the possibility of institutionalizing democratic expression, to show that there is nothing in a democratic politics that precludes the building of institutions. If such institutions are to be built, they will have to arise as a result of struggle itself. Just as, *contra* Rancière, it cannot be determined at the theoretical level whether or not democratic institutions can arise from democratic struggle, neither can it be determined by theory how these institutions might arise or what they might look like. Here theory gives way to practice. It is only in the course of particular democratic struggles that institutions will arise. Their character will be dictated by the context in which that struggle occurs: specific dominations confronted with specific expressions of equality. One cannot dictate in advance the *substantial form* a community of equals might take. One can only recommend in advance a Foucauldian vigilance regarding the possible effects of attempts at institutionalization. Because all the effects of struggle, or of any historical event, cannot be predicted, the project of building institutions must carry with it an attitude, an ethos, of reflection, in order to be mindful of the inegalitarian moments or results of democratic efforts.

If we cannot determine in advance whether or not democratic institutions can arise or be sustained, can we say anything about their likelihood? If theory must remain mute here, will history offer us any lessons? The historical record on institutions of radical democracy is thin. This is not surprising, since elites have no interest in allowing models of thriving democratic institutions. This would make their role superfluous and their wealth and power appear even more obviously undeserved. We cannot look at the histories of liberal or Marxist states, since neither provides a model of egalitarian institutions. The most promising place to investigate would be in the history of anarchist politics, since that is where radical egalitarianism has been taken seriously. And yet anarchism has remained marginal in the history of political struggle.

Perhaps the most sustained effort at building democratic political institutions was in the anarchist labor movement in Spain during the late nineteenth and early twentieth centuries. Murray Bookchin details the history of this effort in his exhaustive and sympathetic *The Spanish Anarchists*.[58] While a discussion of the specifics of this history is beyond our scope, what is clear is that democratic institutions are difficult to maintain for at least two reasons: external pressure and internal discord. The external pressure was provided by factory owners and the state. The doggedness with which the Spanish authorities sought to suppress democratic expression for the five decades or so of the Spanish anarchist movement is testimony to the threat that movement posed to capitalism and to the state. To be sure, the violence of certain quarters of that movement provided a pretext for suppression. However, the very project of building institutions where everyone has an equal say in their administration was inimical to both owners and politicians, who found themselves displaced by projects of the self-management of factory workers and the self-governance of townships, especially in Catalonia.

The suppression of the authorities was often matched by dissonance within the Spanish anarchist movement. First, although this was not strictly internal to the anarchist movement, there was conflict, periodically violent, between anarchists and communists. At times it seemed as though this conflict had higher stakes than the struggle against their common enemy. In addition, there were internal disagreements about the use of violence, the structure of administrative organizations (whether they should be by trade or by geographical area), and the tactics of struggle. Since everyone had an equal say in these debates, the means of their resolution was often unclear. The result of this is that splinter groups formed that had conflicting agendas and approaches. (It is probably worth noting that the problem of resolving internal conflict remains an issue among anarchist activists today. At meetings I have attended, there is a recognition that there is a limit to the effectiveness of seeking universal consensus, and at the same time a discomfort at making decisions by means of voting, which seems to suppress the voices of dissenters.)

These difficulties aside, the Spanish anarchists succeeded, to a remarkable degree, in building ongoing administrative structures: institutions.[59] These institutions were often built among the poorest working classes, thus reinforcing Rancière's view of the equality of intelligence. In this sense, the lesson of Spanish anarchism is precisely one of ambiguity. There seems no reason to assume at the outset that egalitarian institutions cannot be built. On the other hand, there are formidable difficulties in erecting them, and whether they can be sustained is an open question and offers reason for sobriety if not pessimism.

Faced with this sobriety, what is the role of a democratic politics? Is it forced to choose between the unpalatable alternatives of a futile romantic embrace of equality and reformist tinkering? Those who have read this far will see that a democratic politics lies beyond this debate. We may characterize it this way: democratic politics opens the way for reform with more radical ideas. Because domination is multifarious, there are a variety of struggles that can improve a given police order. These struggles introduce reforms, reforms that should not be dismissed simply because they leave other inegalitarian social structures intact. The civil rights movement, for all its failings, succeeded in making life better for many Americans of African descent. On the other hand, what these reformist struggles have in common, if they are democratic in the sense we have articulated, is an active expression of equality that is anything but reformist. This active expression of equality envisions a *community of equals*, a gathering of equally intelligent people conducting lives in common. These lives are neither the fulfillment of roles allotted by a police order nor chaotic expressions of passing individual fancy. They are, or would be, or perhaps could be, lives whose meaning arises from participation in a commonality without identity, a subjectification without subjection. The vision of such lives is already a threat to any police order, and even where it cannot be realized, a democratic politics, in its very activity, keeps this vision before us.

Where does this leave the passive equality we discussed in the first chapter? What is the role of passive equality? Will politics never have done with it? It cannot be said. As with the question of institutions, and inextricable from it, the question of whether a democratic politics can ever overcome the passive equality of liberalism is an open one. It may well be that reforming passive equality with periodic expressions of active equality is the best we can achieve. Otherwise put, it may be that the larger institutions of society will be at best liberal, and that a democratic politics can improve but not alter them. Whether this is the case can only be answered by the practices of democratic politics, not in the pages of this or any other book.

We have tried to construct here, not a politics itself, but a way of thinking about it. What Rancière's thought offers us are not tools for organizing, but a sketch (which I have attempted to build upon) of a politics that responds to the passivity of our current politics. Thought alone does not organize politics, but politics without thought is as dangerous an endeavor as can be imagined. The current state of politics offers us reminders of this on a daily basis. The project, for those of us for whom the current police order is (as Foucault would say) intolerable, is to express in our practices the equality that this framework allows us to presuppose. Where this will lead, and how we will lead ourselves there, is both our challenge and our opportunity. What we must ensure is that we do not cede that challenge and that opportunity to those who would be more than happy to take them up on our behalf.

Notes

1. Rancière often insists that the tradition of political philosophy is addressed to those who have a part rather than those who do not. See, for instance, *The Philosopher and His Poor*.
2. Rancière, *Disagreement*, p. 88.
3. Rancière, *On the Shores of Politics*, p. 49.
4. For empirical substantiation of this, see Richard Layard's *Happiness: Lessons from a New Science*. New York: Penguin Books, 2005.
5. Rancière, *Disagreement*, pp. 101–2.
6. Rancière, *On the Shores of Politics*, p. 35.
7. For an early history of European and U.S. neoliberalism stemming from German ordoliberalism, see Michel Foucault's 1978–79 lecture series at the Collège de France, *Naissance de la biopolitique*. Paris: Gallimard, 2004.
8. Rancière, *On the Shores of Politics*, p. 14.
9. Rancière, *La Haine de la démocratie*, p. 87.
10. To be sure, the representatives in the European Parliament are directly elected by the people, but they are far removed from the concerns that animate the electorate.
11. Rancière, *Disagreement*, pp. 124–5 (translation modified).
12. Rancière, *Disagreement*, p. 135.

13. Emmanuel Levinas, *Totality and Infinity: An Essay on Exteriority*. Tr. Alphonso Lingis. Pittsburgh: Duquesne University Press, 1969 (or. pub. 1961), pp. 22–3.
14. Levinas, *Totality and Infinity*, p. 49.
15. Levinas, *Totality and Infinity*, p. 303.
16. There are theoretical problems as well, connected with the idea of being obliged to something infinitely other to me. I discuss these problems in Chapter 2 of *Reconsidering Difference: Nancy, Derrida, Levinas, and Deleuze*.
17. Levinas, *Totality and Infinity*, p. 43.
18. Levinas, *Totality and Infinity*, p. 304.
19. Rancière, *Disagreement*, p. 136.
20. Jacques Rancière, *Malaise dans l'esthétique*. Paris: Galilée, 2004, p. 155.
21. See, for example, Rancière, *Malaise dans l'esthétique*, pp. 119–41.
22. Jacques Rancière, *Chroniques des temps consensuels*. Paris: Éditions du Seuil, 2005, p. 130.
23. Rancière, *Chroniques*, p. 130.
24. See, for instance, Lyotard's *Heidegger and "the Jews"*, tr. Andreas Michel and Mark Roberts. Minneapolis: University of Minnesota Press, 1990 (or. pub. 1988); Adorno's *Negative Dialectics*, tr. E. B. Ashton. New York: Seabury Press, 1973 (or. pub. 1966), esp. pp. 361–5; Derrida's *Of Spirit: Heidegger and the Question*, tr. Geoffrey Bennington and Rachel Bowlby. Chicago: University of Chicago Press, 1989 (or. pub. 1987); Nancy and Lacoue-Labarthe's "The Nazi Myth," tr. Brian Holmes, *Critical Inquiry*, Vol. 16, No. 2, Winter 1990, pp. 291–312; and Lacoue-Labarthe's *Heidegger, Art and Politics*, tr. Chris Turner. Oxford: Basil Blackwell, 1990 (or. pub. 1988). With the exception of Adorno, the focus of these thinkers on the Holocaust is precipitated by "the Heidegger affair," which followed upon the French publication of Victor Farías' *Heidegger and Nazism*, tr. Joseph Margolis and Tom Rockmore. Philadelphia: Temple University Press, 1989 (or. pub. 1987). Although there were no new revelations in this book about Heidegger's involvement with the Nazis, its publication caused a sensation that forced those who were engaged with Heidegger's thought to grapple with the meaning of this involvement.
25. Rancière, *Malaise*, pp. 157–9.
26. Rancière, *Malaise*, p. 151.
27. http://www.whitehouse.gov/news/releases/2001/09/20010920-8.html
28. Rancière, *La haine de la démocratie*, pp. 9–10.
29. Rancière, *La haine de la démocratie*, p. 26.
30. Rancière points out, however, that this view of equality and inequality, while new with respect to capitalism, harkens back to Plato, for whom the people were driven solely by needs and thus needed to be governed by a capable elite. See *La haine de la démocratie*, pp. 41–4.

31. See, for instance, Milton Friedman's January 11, 1998 *New York Times* editorial, "There's No Justice in the War on Drugs."
32. Rancière, *Malaise*, pp. 158–9.
33. Rancière, *Malaise*, p. 149.
34. Rancière, *On the Shores of Politics*, p. 11 (translation modified).
35. *La Haine de la démocratie*, p. 106.
36. For more on this, see my book *Our Practices, Our Selves*. University Park, PA: Penn State Press, 2001.
37. I owe this point to discussion with Professor Mark Lance, from Georgetown University.
38. For an excellent discussion of the roots of the political appeal to fear, see Corey Robin's *Fear: The History of a Political Idea*. Oxford: Oxford University Press, 2004.
39. His says this several times, for instance in an interview with PBS at http://www.pbs.org/wnet/newyork/series/interview/gray.html.
40. *Chronique des temps consensuels*, p. 8.
41. For more on the use of local traditions in Zapatista organizational efforts, see Lynn Stephen's *Zapatista Lives!: Histories and Cultural Politics in Southern Mexico*. Berkeley, CA: University of California Press, 2002.
42. Ex., Masao Miyoshi, "A Borderless World? From Colonialism to Transnationalism and the Decline of the Nation-State," *Critical Inquiry*, Vol. 19, No. 4, Summer 1993, pp. 726–51.
43. Cambridge, MA: Harvard University Press, 2000
44. Rancière, *La Haine de la démocratie*, pp. 85–6.
45. Rancière, *La Haine de la démocratie*, pp. 90–1.
46. Hannah Arendt, *The Origins of Totalitarianism*. New York: Harcourt, Brace and Co., 1951, p. 288.
47. Arendt, *The Origins of Totalitarianism*, p. 294.
48. Jacques Rancière, "Who Is the Subject of the Rights of Man?" *The South Atlantic Quarterly*, 103.2/3, 2004, p. 307.
49. Rancière, "Who Is the Subject of the Rights of Man?", p. 307.
50. Rancière, "Who Is the Subject of the Rights of Man?", p. 309.
51. Rancière, "Who Is the Subject of the Rights of Man?", p. 304.
52. See http://www.indymedia.com/mc/index.php.
53. For information on Critical Mass, see http://en.wikipedia.org/wiki/Critical_Mass.
54. Rancière, *On the Shores of Politics*, p. 84.
55. Studs Terkel's *Working* (New York: Pantheon, 1974) provides an insightful set of interviews of how people feel about and deal with their working lives.
56. Among the few reflections on friendship in the philosophical literature, Aristotle's thoughts in the eighth and ninth books of the *Nichomachean Ethics* still stand as a model, if not of friendship itself then at least of a rigorous and sensitive approach to it.

57. Robert Putnam, *Bowling Alone: The Collapse and Revival of American Community*. New York: Simon and Schuster, 2001.
58. Murray Bookchin, *The Spanish Anarchists*.
59. See, for instance, the structure of the *Confederacion Nacional del Trabajo* (the CNT) in Chapter 8 of *The Spanish Anarchists*.

Bibliography

Adorno, Theodor. *Negative Dialectics*, tr. E. B. Ashton. New York: Seabury Press, 1973 (or. pub. 1966).

Althusser, Louis et al. (eds). *Lire le Capital*. Paris: Maspéro, 1965.

Appiah, Kwame Anthony. "Identity, Authenticity, Survival: Multicultural Societies and Social Reproduction," in Charles Taylor, et al. *Multiculturalism*. Princeton, NJ: Princeton University Press, 1994.

Arendt, Hannah. *The Origins of Totalitarianism*. New York: Harcourt, Brace and Co., 1951.

Aristotle. *The Politics*. tr. T. A. Sinclair, rev. Trevor J. Saunders. London: Penguin Books, 1981.

Badiou, Alain. "Rancière and Apolitics," in *Metapolitics*. tr. Jason Barker. London: Verso, 2005 (or. pub. 1998).

Bakunin, Michael. *God and the State*. New York: Dover Publications, 1970 (or. pub. 1882).

Bakunin, Michael. *Statism and Anarchy*, tr. and ed. Marshall S. Shatz. Cambridge: Cambridge University Press, 1990.

Bookchin, Murray. "The Forms of Freedom," and "Post-Scarcity Anarchism," in *Post-Scarcity Anarchism*, 3rd ed., Edinburgh: AK Press, 2004 (or. pub. 1970).

Bookchin, Murray. *The Spanish Anarchists: The Heroic Years 1868–1936*. New York: Free Life Editions, 1977.

Branch, Taylor. *Parting the Waters: America in the King Years 1954–63*. New York: Simon and Schuster, 1988.

Brandom, Robert. *Making it Explicit*. Cambridge, MA: Harvard University Press, 1994.

Critical Mass. http://en.wikipedia.org/wiki/Critical_Mass

Crowder, George. *Classical Anarchism: The Political Thought of Godwin, Proudhon, Bakunin, and Kropotkin*. Oxford: Clarendon Press, 1991.

Deleuze, Gilles and Foucault, Michel. "Intellectuals and Power," in Michel Foucault, *Language, Counter-Memory, Practice: Selected Essays and Interviews*. ed. Donald F. Bouchard, tr. Donald F. Bouchard and Sherry Simon. Ithaca, NY: Cornell University Press, 1977 (or. pub. 1972).

Deleuze, Gilles. *Nietzsche and Philosophy*. tr. Hugh Tomlinson. New York: Columbia University Press, 1983 (or. pub. 1962).

Deleuze, Gilles. *Spinoza: Practical Philosophy*. tr. Robert Hurley. San Francisco: City Light Books, 1988 (or. pub. 1970).

Derrida, Jacques. *Of Spirit: Heidegger and the Question*, tr. Geoffrey Bennington and Rachel Bowlby. Chicago: University of Chicago Press, 1989 (or. pub. 1987).

Farías, Victor. *Heidegger and Nazism*, tr. Joseph Margolis and Tom Rockmore. Philadelphia: Temple University Press, 1989 (or. pub. 1987).

Foucault, Michel. *The Archaeology of Knowledge*. tr. A. M. Sheridan Smith. New York: Harper and Row, 1972 (or. pub. 1969).

Foucault, Michel. *Discipline and Punish: The Birth of the Prison*. New York: Random House, 1977 (or. pub. 1975).

Foucault, Michel, "The Ethic of Care for the Self as a Practice of Freedom" (an interview), in James Bernauer and David Rasmussen. *The Final Foucault*. Cambridge, MA: MIT Press, 1988.

Foucault, Michel. *The History of Sexuality, Vol. 1: An Introduction*. tr. Robert Hurley. New York: Random House, 1978 (or. pub. 1976).

Foucault, Michel. *Naissance de la biopolitique*. Paris: Gallimard, 2004.

Foucault, Michel. "Omnes et Singulatum," http://www.tannerlectures.utah.edu/lectures/foucault81.pdf

Foucault, Michel. "Politics and Ethics: An Interview," tr. Catherine Porter, in Paul Rabinow. *The Foucault Reader*. New York: Pantheon, 1984.

Foucault, Michel. *Sécurité, territoire, population: Cours au Collège de France (1977–1978)*. Paris: Gallimard, 2004.

Friedman, Milton. "There's No Justice in the War on Drugs," *The New York Times,* January 11, 1998.

Gilligan, Carol. *In a Different Voice: Psychological Theory and Women's Development*. Cambridge, MA: Harvard University Press, 1982.

Goldman, Emma. "Anarchism," in *Anarchism and Other Essays*. New York: Dover Publications, 1969 (or. 3rd ed. published 1917).

Gray, Spalding. http://www.pbs.org/wnet/newyork/series/interview/gray.html

Hardt, Michael and Negri, Antonio. *Empire*. Cambridge, MA: Harvard University Press, 2000.

Hoover, Judith D. and Howard, Leigh Anne. "The Political Correctness Controversy Revisited: Retreat from Argumentation and Reaffirmation of Critical Dialogue," in *American Behavioral Scientist*, Vol. 38, No. 7, June/July 1995, pp. 963–75.

Hume, David. *A Treatise of Human Nature*. 2nd ed. Oxford: Clarendon Press, 1978 (or. pub. 1739).

Indymedia.http://www.indymedia.com/mc/index.php

Joll, James. *The Anarchists*. 2nd ed. Cambridge, MA: Harvard University Press, 1980.

Kant, Immanuel. *Groundwork of the Metaphysic of Morals*, tr. H. J. Paton. New York: Harper & Row, 1956.

Kropotkin, Peter. "Anarchism" (article for *Encyclopedia Britannica*), in Peter

Kropotkin, *The Conquest of Bread and Other Writings*, ed. Marshall S. Shatz. Cambridge: Cambridge University Press, 1995 (essay or. pub. 1910).

Kropotkin, Peter. "Anarchist Morality" and "Modern Science and Anarchism," in *Kroptokin's Revolutionary Pamphlets: A Collection of Writings*, ed. Roger N. Baldwin. New York: Dover Publications, Inc., 1927 (or. pub. 1909).

Kropotkin, Peter. *Mutual Aid: A Factor of Evolution*, ed. Paul Avrich. New York: New York University Press, 1972 (or. pub. 1902).

Kuhn, Thomas. *The Structure of Scientific Revolutions*. Chicago: University of Chicago Press, 1962.

Lacoue-Labarthe, Philippe. *Heidegger, Art and Politics*, tr. Chris Turner. Oxford: Basil Blackwell, 1990 (or. pub. 1988).

Layard, Richard. *Happiness: Lessons from a New Science*. New York: Penguin Books, 2005.

Lefort, Claude. "Politics and Human Rights," tr. Alan Sheridan, in Claude Lefort, *The Political Forms of Modern Society*, ed. John B. Thompson. Cambridge, MA: MIT Press, 1986.

Levinas, Emmanuel. *Totality and Infinity: An Essay on Exteriority,* tr. Alphonso Lingis. Pittsburgh: Duquesne University Press, 1969 (or. pub. 1961).

Lyotard, Jean-François. *Heidegger and "the Jews"*, tr. Andreas Michel and Mark Roberts. Minneapolis: University of Minnesota Press, 1990 (or. pub. 1988).

Marx, Karl and Engels, Friedrich. *The Communist Manifesto*, in Lawrence Simon. *Karl Marx: Selected Writings*. Indianapolis: Hackett, 1994 (essay or. pub. 1848).

Marx, Karl. "On the Jewish Question," in Karl Marx, *Early Writings*. tr. Rodney Livingston and Gregor Benton. New York: Vintage, 1975.

May, Todd. *Between Genealogy and Epistemology: Psychology, Politics, and Knowledge in the Thought of Michel Foucault*. University Park, PA: Penn State Press, 1993.

May, Todd. *The Moral Theory of Poststructuralism*, University Park, PA: Penn State Press, 1995.

May, Todd. *Our Practices, Our Selves*. University Park, PA: Penn State Press, 2001.

May, Todd. *The Political Philosophy of Poststructuralist Anarchism*. University Park, PA: Penn State Press, 1994.

May, Todd. *Reconsidering Difference: Nancy, Derrida, Levinas, and Deleuze*. University Park, PA: Penn State Press, 1997.

Miyoshi, Masao. "A Borderless World? From Colonialism to Transnationalism and the Decline of the Nation-State," *Critical Inquiry*, Vol. 19, No. 4, Summer 1993, pp. 726–51.

Nancy, Jean-Luc and Lacoue-Labarthe, Philippe. "The Nazi Myth," tr. Brian Holmes, *Critical Inquiry*, Vol. 16, No. 2, Winter 1990, pp. 291–312.

Nietzsche, Friedrich. *On the Genealogy of Morals*. tr. Douglass Smith. Oxford: Oxford University Press, 1996 (or. pub. 1887).

Nozick, Robert. *Anarchy, State, and Utopia*. New York: Basic Books, 1974.

Plato. *Republic,* tr. G. M. A. Grube, rev. C. D. C. Reeve. Indianapolis: Hackett, 1992.

Proudhon, Joseph-Pierre. *On the Political Capacity of the Working Class*, cited in *Selected Writings of P.-J. Proudhon*, ed. Stewart Edwards, tr. Elizabeth Fraser. New York: Doubleday and Co., 1969 (or. pub. 1865).

Putnam, Robert. *Bowling Alone: The Collapse and Revival of American Community*. New York: Simon & Schuster, 2001.

Rancière, Jacques. *Aux bords du politique*. Paris: Gallimard, 1998.

Rancière, Jacques. *Chroniques des temps consensuels*. Paris: Éditions du Seuil, 2005.

Rancière, Jacques. "The Concept of 'Critique' and the 'Critique of Political Economy'," in *Ideology, Method, and Marx: Essays from* Economy and Society, ed. Ali Rattansi. London: Routledge, 1989.

Rancière, Jacques. *Disagreement*. tr. Julie Rose. Minneapolis: University of Minnesota Press, 1999 (or. pub. 1995).

Rancière, Jacques. *La Haine de la démocratie*. Paris: La fabrique editions, 2005.

Rancière, Jacques. *The Ignorant Schoolmaster, Five Lessons in Intellectual Emancipation*, tr. Krisin Ross. Stanford, CA: Stanford University Press, 1991 (or. pub. 1987).

Rancière, Jacques. *La Leçon d'Althusser*. Paris: Gallimard, 1974.

Rancière, Jacques. *Malaise dans l'esthétique*. Paris: Galilée, 2004.

Rancière, Jacques. *La Mésentente: Politique et philosophie*. Paris: Galilée, 1995.

Rancière, Jacques. *Nights of Labor: The Worker's Dream in Nineteenth-Century France*, tr. John Drury. Philadelphia: Temple University Press, 1989 (or. pub. 1981).

Rancière, Jacques. *On the Shores of Politics*, tr. Liz Heron. London: Verso, 1995 (or. pub. 1992).

Rancière, Jacques. *The Philosopher and His Poor*. tr. John Drury, Corinne Oster, and Andrew Parker. Durham, NC: Duke University Press, 2004 (or. pub. 1983).

Rancière, Jacques. "Les philosophes san porte-voix," *Libération*, June 25, 2004. www.liberation.fr/imprimer.php?Article=216733

Rancière, Jacques. "Politics, Identification, and Subjectivization," in *The Identity in Question*, ed. John Rajchman, New York: Routledge, 1995.

Rancière, Jacques. "Ten Theses on Politics," *Theory and Event*, Vol. 5, No. 3, 2001.

Rancière, Jacques. "Who is the Subject of the Rights of Man?" *The South Atlantic Quarterly*, 103.2/3, 2004.

Rawls, John. *A Theory of Justice*. Cambridge, MA: Harvard University Press, 1971.

Robin, Cory. *Fear: The History of a Political Idea*. Oxford: Oxford University Press, 2004.

Ross, Kristin. *May '68 and its Afterlives* Chicago: University of Chicago Press, 2002.

Rouse, Joseph. *Engaging Science: How to Understand its Practices Philosophically*. Ithaca, NY: Cornell University Press, 1996.

Rouse, Joseph. *Knowledge and Power: Toward a Political Philosophy of Science*. Ithaca, NY: Cornell University Press, 1990.

Rue, Martin. "Truth, Power, Self: An Interview with Michel Foucault," in Luther H. Martin, Huck Gutman, and Patrick Hutton (eds), *Technologies of the Self*. Amherst, MA: University of Massachusetts Press, 1988 (interview conducted in 1982).

Sellars, Wilfrid. "Empiricism and the Philosophy of Mind," in *Science, Perception, and Reality*. London: Routledge & Kegan Paul, 1963.

Sen, Amartya. "Capability and Well-Being," in *The Quality of Life*, ed. Martha Nussbaum and Amartya Sen. Oxford: Clarendon Press, 1993.

Sen, Amartya. "Equality of What?" in Amartya Sen, *Choice, Welfare and Measurement*. Cambridge, MA: MIT Press, 1982.

Sen, Amartya. *Inequality Reexamined*. Cambridge, MA: Harvard University Press, 1992.

Sen, Amartya. *On Ethics and Economics*. Oxford: Blackwell, 1987.

Sharp, Gene. *Power and Struggle*. Boston: Porter Sargent, 1973.

Stephen, Lynn. *Zapatista Lives!: Histories and Cultural Politics in Southern Mexico*. Berkeley, CA: University of California Press, 2002.

Stiglitz, Joseph. *Globalization and its Discontents*. New York: W.W. Norton, 2002.

Terkel, Studs. *Working*. New York: Pantheon, 1974.

Thomas, Paul. *Karl Marx and the Anarchists*. London: Routledge & Kegan Paul, 1980.

Ward, Colin. *Anarchy in Action*. London: Freedom Press, 1988.

Wieck, David. "The Negativity of Anarchism," in *Reinventing Anarchy*, ed. Howard Ehrlich, Carol Ehrlich, David DeLeon, and Glenda Morris. London: Routledge & Kegan Paul, 1977 (essay or. pub. 1975).

http://www. whitehouse.gov/news/releases/2001/09/20010920-8.html

Williams, Bernard. *Ethics and the Limits of Philosophy*. Cambridge, MA: Harvard University Press, 1985.

Williams, Bernard. "A Critique of Utilitarianism," in J. J. C. Smart and Bernard Williams. *Utilitarianism: For and Against*. Cambridge: Cambridge University Press, 1973.

Wittgenstein, Ludwig. *Culture and Value*, ed. G. H. von Wright, tr. Peter Winch. Chicago: University of Chicago Press, 1980.

194   *The Political Thought of Jacques Rancière*

Young, Iris Marion. *Justice and the Politics of Difference.* Princeton, NJ: Princeton University Press, 1990.
Žižek, Slavoj. "A Leftist Plea for Eurocentrism," *Critical Inquiry*, Vol. 24, No. 4, Summer 1998, pp. 988–1009.

Index